Lucy Johnstone is a consultant clinical psychologist working in Wales, author of *Users and Abusers of Psychiatry* (Routledge, 2nd edition 2000) and co-editor of *Formulation in Psychology and Psychotherapy: Making sense of people's problems* (Routledge, 2nd edition 2013) along with other work taking a critical perspective on mental health theory and practice. She was lead author of the *Good Practice Guidelines for the Use of Psychological Formulation* (Division of Clinical Psychology, 2011).

Do you still need your psychiatric diagnosis? This book will help you to decide.

A revolution is underway in mental health. If the authors of the diagnostic manuals are admitting that psychiatric diagnoses are not supported by evidence, then no one should be forced to accept them. If many mental health workers are openly questioning diagnosis and saying we need a different and better system, then service users and carers should be allowed to do so too. This book is about choice. It is about giving people the information to make up their own minds, and exploring alternatives for those who wish to do so.

STRAIGHT TALKING INTRODUCTIONS TO MENTAL HEALTH PROBLEMS
edited by Richard Bentall and Pete Sanders

Psychiatric Drugs
Joanna Moncrieff

Children's Mental Health Problems
Sami Timimi

Psychological Treatments
David Pilgrim

Caring for Someone with Mental Health Problems
Jen Kilyon & Theresa Smith (eds)

Being a User of Psychiatric Services
Peter Beresford

The Causes of Mental Health Problems
John Read & Pete Sanders

Rather than accept that solutions to mental health problems are owned by the medical professions, these books look at alternatives and provide information so people can make more decisions about their own lives. Becoming more active in mental health issues requires knowledge — this series of books is a starting point for anyone who wants to know more about mental health problems.

Richard Bentall is Professor of Clinical Psychology at the University of Liverpool and previously held chairs in the Universities of Manchester and Bangor. He has carried out research on the causes and treatment of severe psychiatric problems for over 25 years. He is the author of *Madness Explained: Psychosis and human nature* (Penguin, 2003) and *Doctoring the Mind* (Penguin, 2009).

Pete Sanders has been a counsellor, educator, clinical supervisor and author for over 30 years. He has published numerous articles on psychotherapy and mental health, and several books, including *First Steps in Counselling, 4th ed* (PCCS Books, 2011) and *The Person-Centred Counselling Primer* (PCCS Books, 2006).

A Straight Talking Introduction to

Psychiatric Diagnosis

Lucy Johnstone

PCCS BOOKS
Monmouth

First published 2014

PCCS BOOKS Ltd
Wyastone Business Park
Ganarew
MONMOUTH
NP25 3SR
UK
Tel +44 (0)1600 891509
www.pccs-books.co.uk

A Straight Talking Introduction to Psychiatric Diagnosis

A CIP catalogue record for this book is available from the British Library

ISBN 978 1 906254 66 7

Cover designed in the UK by Old Dog Graphics
Typeset in the UK by Raven Books
Printed by Lightning Source

Contents

Acknowledgements

I am very grateful to Mary Boyle, Laura Delano, Jacqui Dillon, Angela Gilchrist, Amanda Hall, Phil Hickey and John Read for their helpful comments …

… and to Eleanor, Fay, Laura, Rachel and Rufus for permission to use their stories.

Introduction to the *Straight Talking* series

What are mental health problems?

Much of what is written and spoken about emotional distress or mental health problems implies that they are illnesses. This can lead us all too easily to believe that we no longer have to think about mental health problems, because illness is best left to doctors. They are the illness experts, and psychiatrists are the doctors who specialise in mental illness. This series of books is different because we don't think that all mental health problems should be automatically regarded as illnesses.

If mental health problems aren't necessarily illnesses, it means that the burden of responsibility for distress in our lives should not be entirely shouldered by doctors and psychiatrists. All citizens have a responsibility, however small, in creating a world where everyone has a decent opportunity to live a fulfilling life. This is a contentious idea, but one which we want to advance alongside the dominant medical view.

Rather than accept that solutions to mental health problems are 'owned' by the medical profession, we will take a good look at alternatives which involve the users of psychiatric services, their carers, families, friends and other 'ordinary people' taking control of their own lives. One of the tools required in order to become active in mental health issues, whether your own or other people's, is knowledge. This series of books is a starting point for anyone who wants to know more about mental health.

How these books are written

We want these books to be understandable, so we use everyday language wherever possible. The books could have been almost completely jargon-free, but we thought that including some technical and medical terms would be helpful. Most doctors, psychiatrists and psychologists use the medical model of mental illness and manuals to help them diagnose mental health problems. The medical model and the diagnostic manuals use a particular set of terms to describe what doctors think of as 'conditions'. Although these words aren't very good at describing individual people's experiences, they are used a lot in psychiatric and psychological services, so we thought it would be helpful to define these terms as we went along and use them in a way that might help readers understand what the professionals mean. We don't expect that psychiatrists and psychologists and others working in mental health services will stop using medical terminology (although we think it might be respectful for them to drop it when talking to their patients and their families), so these books should help you get used to, and learn, *their* language.

The books also contain resources for further learning (pp. 103–18). As well as lists of books, websites and organisations at the end of the book, there are endnotes. These will not be important to everyone, but they do tell the reader where information – a claim about effectiveness, an argument for or against, or a quotation – has come from so you can follow it up if you wish.

Being realistic and reassuring

Our aim is to be realistic – neither overly optimistic nor pessimistic. Things are nearly always more complicated than we would like them to be. Honest evaluations of mental health problems, of what might cause them, of what can help, and of what the likely outcome might be, are, like so much in life, somewhere in between. For the vast majority of people it would be wrong to say that they have an illness from which they will never recover. But it would be equally wrong to say that they will be completely unchanged by the distressing thoughts and feelings they are having. Life is an accumulation of experiences. There is usually no pill, or any other treatment for that matter, that will take us back to 'how we were before'. There are many things we can do (and we will be looking at lots of them in this series) in collaboration with doctors, psychiatrists, psychologists, counsellors, indeed everyone working in mental health services, with the help of our friends and family, or on our own, which stand a good chance of helping us feel better and build a constructive life with hope for the future.

Of course, we understand that the experiences dealt with in these books can sometimes be so overwhelming, confusing and terrifying that people will try to escape from them by withdrawing, going mad or even by trying to kill themselves. This happens when our usual coping strategies fail us. We accept that killing oneself is, in some circumstances, a rational act – that for the person in question it can make a lot of sense. Nonetheless, we believe that much of the distress that underpins such an extreme course of action, from which there can be no turning back, is avoidable. For this reason, all of the books in this series point towards realistic hope and recovery.

Debates

There is no single convenient answer to many of the most important questions explored in these books. No matter how badly we might wish for a simple answer, what we have is a series of debates, or arguments more like, between stakeholders, and there are many stakeholders whose voices demand space in these books. We use the word 'stakeholders' here because service users, carers, friends, family, doctors, psychologists, psychiatrists, nurses and other workers, scientists in drug companies, therapists, indeed all citizens, have a stake in how our society understands and deals with problems of mental health. It is simultaneously big business and intimately personal, and many things in between. As we go along, we try to explain how someone's stake in distress (including our own, where we can see it), whether business or personal, can influence their experience and judgement.

Whilst we want to present competing (sometimes opposing) viewpoints, we don't want to leave the reader high and dry to evaluate complicated debates on their own. We will try to present reasonable conclusions which might point in certain directions for personal action. Above all, though, we believe that knowledge is power and that the better informed you are, even though the information might be conflicting, the more able you will be to make sound decisions.

It's also useful to be reminded that the professionals involved in helping distressed people are themselves caught in the same flow of conflicting information. It is their *job*, however, to interpret it in our service, so that the best solutions are available to as many people as possible. You may have noticed that the word 'best' brings with it certain challenges, not least of all, what we mean when we use this term. Perhaps the best means the most effective?

However, even using words like 'effective' doesn't completely clear up the puzzle. An effective treatment could be the one which returns someone to work quickly, if you are an employer; or one which makes someone feel happier and more calm, if they are your son or daughter. Readers will also know from recent press coverage that the National Institute for Health and Care Excellence (NICE), which evaluates and recommends treatments, keeps one eye on the budget, so 'effective' might mean 'cost effective' to some people. This brings us to evidence.

Evidence

Throughout these books there will be material which we will present as 'evidence'. This is one of the most contentious terms to be found in this series. One person's evidence is another person's fanciful mythology and yet another person's oppressive propaganda. Nevertheless the term crops up increasingly in everyday settings, most relevantly when we hear of 'evidence-based practice'. The idea behind this term is that the treatments psychologists and psychiatrists offer should be those that work. Crudely put, there should be some evidence that, say, talking about problems, or taking a prescribed drug, actually helps people to feel better. We encounter a real problem, however, when trying to evaluate this evidence, as the books will demonstrate. We will try not to discount any 'evidence' out of hand, but we will evaluate it, and we will do this with a bias towards scientific evaluation.

The types of evidence that will be covered in these books, along with their positive and negative points, include the following.

Research methods, numbers and statistics

On the one hand, the logic of most research is simple, but on the other hand, the way things have to be arranged to avoid bias in the results can lead to a perplexing system of measurements. Even the experts lose the sense of it sometimes. Authors will try to explain the logic of studies, but almost certainly leave out the details. You can look these up yourself if you wish.

The books in this series look at research into a wide range of issues regarding mental health problems, including the experience of distress, what is known about the causes of problems, and their prevention and treatment. Different research methods are more or less appropriate for each of these areas, so we will be looking at different types of research as we go along. We say this now because many readers may be most familiar with studies into the *effective treatments* of distress, and we want to emphasise that there are many credible and valid sources of essential information about distress that are sometimes overlooked.

You may have come across the idea that some research methods are 'better' than others – that they constitute a 'gold standard'. In the case of research into the effectiveness of different treatments, the gold standard is usually considered to be 'randomised controlled trials' (RCTs). In simple terms, RCTs are complex (and often very expensive) experiments in which a group of individuals who all suffer from the same problem are randomly allocated to a treatment or a 'control' condition (at its simplest, no treatment at all) to see whether the treatment works. We are not necessarily convinced that RCTs always *are* the best way of conducting research into effective treatments, but they are, at the present time, the method given most credence by bodies which control funding, such as the National Health Service's National Institute of Health and Care Excellence, so we need to understand them.

Personal experience

Personal experience is an important source of evidence to the extent that, nowadays, people who have suffered debilitating psychiatric distress are sometimes called 'experts by experience'. Personal stories provide an essential counterbalance to the impersonal numbers and statistics often found in research projects such as RCTs. Whilst not everyone is average, by definition, most people are. Balancing the average results obtained from RCTs with some personal stories helps complete the picture and is now widely accepted to the extent that it has given birth to the new field of 'survivor research'.

Understanding contexts

Widening our view to include the families and lives of people and the cultural, economic, social and political settings in which we live completes the picture. Mental health problems are connected to the conditions in which we all live, just as much as they are connected to our biology. From the start we want readers to know that, if there is one message or model which the books are trying to get across, it is that problems in mental health are more often than not the result of complex events in the environments in which we live and our reactions to them. These reactions can also be influenced by our biology or the way we have learned to think and feel. Hopefully these books will help disentangle the puzzle of distress and provide positive suggestions and hope for us all, whether we work in the system, currently have mental health problems ourselves, are caring for someone, or are friends with someone who has.

We hope that readers of these books will feel empowered by what they learn, and thereby more able to get the best out of mental health services. It would be wonderful if our efforts, directly or indirectly, influence the development of services that effectively address the emotional, social and practical needs of people with mental health problems.

Richard Bentall
Pete Sanders
April 2009

Chapter 1
What this book aims to do

Like the other books in this series, this one aims to provide
information and clarification so that service users, carers,
professionals and anyone else with an interest in mental
health will be better placed to make choices about their own
beliefs and practices. Even if we have no involvement with
mental health services at present, any of us might need to
support a relative or friend or find help for ourselves at some
point in the future. In the controversial and complex subject
of psychiatric diagnosis, we all need to be as well-informed as
possible.

To give a bit of personal background, I have worked
in adult mental health services for many years, alternating
with academic posts. I am also the author of a book (*Users
and Abusers of Psychiatry*, Routledge, 2000) and a number
of chapters and articles taking a critical perspective on
psychiatry. As such, my own conclusion, based on extensive
reading and clinical work and many enlightening discussions
with service users, is that psychiatric diagnosis is not a valid
or evidence-based way of understanding the difficulties and
distress that people experience.

When I first started working in mental health, such
statements were considered to be the mark of some kind of
extremist. Things are changing rapidly in psychiatry, and part
of the reason for this book is that similar views are now being
widely expressed, even by some members of the psychiatric
establishment. An even more important issue is the impact of

psychiatric diagnosis on the users of psychiatric services, and on the way they see themselves and their problems. People who have been diagnosed have mixed views. There are some advantages to acquiring a diagnostic label, including being able to access services and claim benefits. However, there is evidence that their overall effect is unhelpful, and sometimes very damaging.

This whole area inspires such strong feelings that I want to emphasise immediately that *mental distress is very real.* Of course people do suffer from terrifying, overwhelming and often disabling experiences such as hearing hostile voices, feeling so despairing that they want to kill themselves, being paralysed by anxiety, swinging from high to low moods, and so on. It is hard to imagine anything worse than going through the hell of a mental breakdown – although watching a loved one who is in this torment must come pretty close.

It is necessary to spell this out because as a society, we seem to find it hard to find a middle ground between 'You have a physical illness, and therefore your distress is real and no one is to blame for it' and 'Your difficulties are imaginary and/or your or someone else's fault, and you ought to pull yourself together'. As soon as anyone raises questions about diagnosis, people tend to assume that someone is being blamed, or that service users are having their distress denied. And as soon as this happens, strong feelings are stirred up on all sides and the important issues quickly get lost in angry accusations and counter-accusations.

I hope that this book will show that there can be a sensitive and realistic view which lies somewhere in between the very unhelpful, black-or-white positions sometimes described as 'brain or blame',[1] or in an American version, 'chemistry or character'.[2] We need to acknowledge people's suffering and lack of control in many areas of their lives, while at the same time building on their strengths so that they can,

2

with the right support, move towards recovery. For all sorts of complex reasons, this seems to be a very difficult balance to achieve.

So, in this book, I will be raising questions about the idea that mental health problems can best be explained as a kind of medical illness. However, I will *not* be doubting in any way the enormous struggle to survive and recover from these devastating difficulties. Nor will I be seeking to lay blame at anyone's door. As evidenced by the personal stories later in the book, with the right kind of information and support, people can stop seeing themselves as victims of a disease process and can overcome even the deepest anguish and despair. This process has to start with the most accurate and helpful description of the problems themselves.

What this book is designed to help people to think about is the currently dominant theory that these experiences *are best understood as a kind of 'illness' which needs a medical diagnosis.* Is giving someone a psychiatric diagnosis the best way of answering the question of why they are suffering in this way? What evidence do we have for this kind of explanation? And could there be different kinds of understanding that are more helpful? I am not questioning the reality of the chaos and despair. Rather, I am questioning the explanation that a diagnosis claims to offer, and suggesting that there may be other, more accurate and useful ways of making sense of people's distress.

I am making this clear so that readers can assess my arguments accordingly. No one comes from a neutral position on these issues, and everyone's views need to be subjected to scrutiny and debate, not accepted as undisputed fact. There are many powerful vested interests in preserving the diagnostic system, not least the pharmaceutical companies whose influence is felt in every area of mental health work. Diagnosis also serves, or seems to serve, the purposes of

3

deciding on responsibility in the criminal justice system, determining access to benefits and insurance cover, planning services and so on.[3] It has been argued too that locating the results of social problems (unemployment, poor housing, deprivation and inequality, etc.) within individuals serves the interests of governments and policy-makers.[4]

All of this may explain why the debate about psychiatric diagnosis is one of the most heated in the whole of medicine. Professionals who dare to question diagnosis are frequently accused of ignorance, divisiveness, promoting their own selfish personal or professional interests, deliberately attacking other professions, diverting attention from the task of helping patients, blaming parents, engaging in childish squabbling, denying people's suffering, and so on. This is a sure sign that there is more going on than a straightforward scientific debate about the evidence. Whatever motives people may or may not have, the arguments need to be assessed on their own merits. I hope this book will equip readers to do this.

The debate is likely to arouse the strongest reactions in service users and carers, for very understandable reasons. It is always hard to be faced with views that might require a very fundamental shift in how you see yourself and your difficulties, especially when you have accepted (as we all tend to do) an expert opinion that may have had a profound impact on your identity, relationships and whole life. Even if the role of 'mental patient' that follows from a diagnosis has been damaging, it may at least be a familiar one, with some advantages. Towards the end of the book, we will be looking at personal accounts by people who know very well how hard it can be to step out of this role, as well as how doing so can open up new hope for the future.

So, we are entering an area of lively but often intense and angry debate. In such an atmosphere, rational perspectives and uncomfortable facts can easily get lost, and the voices of people who actually use services can get drowned out. You have been warned!

The central message of this book is that within the current state of psychiatry, accepting psychiatric diagnosis as an explanation of someone's difficulties should be a *choice*. People in receipt of a diagnosis may have to go along with it for some official purposes, but I believe that service users have the right and the need to make their own decisions about how they prefer to understand their distress and whether or not they want to take on a diagnosis as part of this.

If, after careful consideration of the pros and cons and the various arguments and alternatives, diagnosis is the view that makes most sense to you as a service user, all well and good. Your relationship with the mental health system will, in some ways, be an easier one, because you will not find yourself in conflict with its basic assumptions.

If diagnosis is not how you prefer to see your difficulties, there are alternatives, as I hope to show towards the end of the book. However, you should be aware that taking them up is likely to be strongly opposed in some quarters. It may even be dismissed as 'lack of insight' (a lack that is, ironically, shared by many mental health professionals). There is no easy answer to this problem, but I have suggested some strategies and resources in Chapter 9. In my view, both choices – to accept or not to accept a diagnosis – should be respected and supported.

There is, of course, a bigger question about whether professionals should be using or offering psychiatric diagnosis at all. If we accept the argument that these are not valid or evidence-based terms, then professionals should be rejecting them in the same way that they have abandoned earlier labels such as 'possession by evil spirits' (in Biblical times) or 'wandering womb' (frequently applied to unhappy Victorian women). This is, I believe, where psychiatry is heading, as discussed in the next chapter. The key issue is whether we are simply going to come up with a new set of diagnostic terms, a bit like replacing the insulting word 'idiot' with 'learning difficulties', or whether we need a completely different way of understanding why people break down. In other words, do we need to get away from the 'disease' model entirely, along with all the language that implies it?

In the meantime, it is important to be aware that it is perfectly possible to work with people in severe mental distress without using psychiatric diagnosis. Many clinical psychologists, including myself, have done this for years, and there are numerous projects both within and outside services which place very little emphasis on diagnostic labels, or else do not use them at all. Supporters of the diagnostic approach are quick to say, 'But we don't have any valid alternatives.' This is simply not true.

It will not be possible to cover all these issues in detail in this book, but I have included references and resources for those who wish to find out more for themselves at the end of Chapter 9.

Psychiatric diagnosis is a very complex subject, and some of the book may be challenging to read. However, with perseverance, I hope that service-user readers will end up with some answers to these important questions:

- What are the problems with psychiatric diagnosis?

- How has diagnosis been helpful and/or unhelpful to me?

- Do I want to accept my diagnosis?

- If I don't want to accept my diagnosis … How else can I understand my difficulties?

- If I don't want to accept my diagnosis … Where can I find support with this decision?

In addition, I hope that friends, families and professionals will have a clearer idea of the issues at stake, and will be better placed to support service users in their preferred way forward.

Some notes

A word about language: I try to avoid terms such as 'illness', 'disorder', 'symptom', 'patient' and so on, because they assume a medical viewpoint. Terms like 'distress', 'experience' and 'service user' are not entirely satisfactory, but they are more neutral.

A word about children's difficulties: Exactly the same principles apply in relation to the problems that are often labelled 'ADHD' (attention deficit hyperactivity disorder) and so on. For further discussion, see *A Straight Talking Introduction to Children's Mental Health Problems* by Sami Timimi.[5]

And a word about professions: People frequently get confused about the difference between psychiatrists and psychologists. Psychiatrists are medical doctors who do the usual five-year training at medical school, and then go on to specialise in mental health. They are able to prescribe medication, and generally see diagnosis as essential, even if they admit that it has flaws. Clinical psychologists, like myself, do a degree in psychology and a three-year postgraduate training. They offer various types of counselling and talking therapy, including CBT (cognitive behavioural therapy). Many, although not all, are critical of the use of psychiatric diagnosis.

The debate about psychiatric diagnosis has been unhelpfully described in some quarters as a dispute between professions. This is not true. Historically, it has always been psychiatrists themselves who have been the most outspoken critics.[6,7,8,9] There are also critics within social work,[10,11] nursing[12] and clinical psychology.[13,14] In other words, critics come from minority groups within and across all professions, as well as from sections of the service user/survivor movement. The central issue, as I hope to show, is about particular *ways of thinking*, not about professions as such. As the next chapter describes, it is a way of thinking that is currently attracting more criticism than ever before.

Chapter 2
Psychiatric diagnosis: The current context

Something extraordinary has been happening in the world of mental health. Readers may be aware that the controversy about psychiatric diagnosis, usually only of interest within the field, has actually reached the general public. Dramatic headlines such as these were seen in the national press in Britain on 2nd February 2012:

> Lonely? Shy? Sad? Well now you're 'mentally ill' too.
> (*The Independent*)

> The proposals in *DSM-5* are likely to shrink the pool of normality to a puddle with more and more people being given a diagnosis of mental illness.
> (Professor Til Wykes, *The Guardian*)

> It is hard to avoid the conclusion that *DSM-5* will help the interests of the drug companies and the wrong-headed belief of some mental health professionals.
> (Professor David Pilgrim, *The Financial Times*)

> Many people who are shy, bereaved, eccentric or have unconventional romantic lives will suddenly find themselves labelled as 'mentally ill'. This isn't valid, isn't true, isn't humane.
> (Professor Peter Kinderman, *The Independent*)

This was accompanied by many other articles in the international press. The trigger for all this was the run-up to the publication of the *Diagnostic and Statistical Manual 5th edition* (known for short as *DSM-5*) in the USA in May 2013.

What is *DSM*?

The *Diagnostic and Statistical Manual of Mental Disorders* is an enormous book of all the possible ways in which someone can be diagnosed with a mental health problem, from schizophrenia to more obscure problems such as trichotillomania (compulsively pulling your hair out). It lists the criteria which determine whether a particular diagnosis is said to apply. It is drawn up by a committee of America's most senior mental health professionals, mainly psychiatrists. The first edition came out in 1952, with 106 disorders. The previous edition, *DSM-IV*, came out in 1994, with a minor updating in 2000 (known as *DSM-IV-TR*, TR standing for 'text revision'). *DSM-5* is thus the first major revision for nearly 20 years, and contains over 400 types of what the manual calls 'mental disorders'.

With each revision, some new categories are added, some existing ones are deleted, and others have their criteria revised in order to try to make the process of diagnosis more accurate. This is an enormously complex, costly and profitable process, involving more than 500 leading clinicians over the last decade. The American Psychiatric Association made an estimated \$100 million a year from *DSM-IV*.[1]

The equivalent European manual is called *ICD*, or the *International Classification of Diseases*, produced by the World Health Organization. It makes up one 'chapter' of a larger volume of medical diseases. It too is revised regularly and we have now reached *ICD-10*, with the 11th edition due in 2017. Criteria for diagnosing particular disorders vary slightly between the two manuals, although a system of 'cross-walking' attempts to match them as closely as possible.

It is important to note that, despite their minor differences, both *DSM* and *ICD* are based on the same set of *principles* – that is, the assumption that mental distress can be divided into categories of medical illnesses or disorders. The arguments in this book therefore apply to both systems. *DSM* is, internationally, the most dominant system, partly because many of the world's most influential journals prefer to publish research studies and award research grants that use its categories. In the USA, insurance companies insist that patients have a formal psychiatric diagnosis in order to be reimbursed for their treatment. This means that diagnosis is much more deeply embedded in the health care system than in the UK, where treatment is free to everyone under the National Health Service.

Even though most psychiatrists do not go running to *DSM* or *ICD* every time they make a diagnosis, and may in fact be quite sceptical about it, it is almost impossible to overestimate its significance. As I will discuss in more depth in Chapter 3, *DSM* and *ICD* are the foundation of psychiatric practice. If the diagnosis isn't correct, or even worse, if the whole idea that people are suffering from some kind of medical illness is flawed, then every other aspect of psychiatric theory and practice is on shaky ground. This accounts for some of the heat in the debate. There is an awful lot at stake.

What are the concerns about *DSM-5*?

The main criticisms of *DSM-5* are:

• The trials that are meant to show that the new or revised categories can be used more accurately than the old ones (sometimes called 'reliability' – discussed further in Chapter 3) have produced very poor results.

• Many categories have been expanded in a way that seems to defy common sense – as the UK headlines suggest. For example, in DSM-IV psychiatrists were encouraged not to diagnose major depression if the person had had a bereavement within the last two months. This already seems a short time to allow for recovery, but the clause has been dropped altogether from DSM-5, leading to widespread fears that normal grief will be seen as a sign of mental illness, and medicated.

• New and bizarre 'illnesses' have been added. Skin-picking, or in its DSM-5 version 'excoriation disorder', may be a bad habit, but is it really a psychiatric illness? Children can be badly behaved, but does it really make sense to diagnose them with disruptive mood dysregulation disorder if they have more than three temper tantrums a week for a year? It is traumatic to be told you have cancer, but if you are more distressed than your doctor thinks you should be, does it really help to be told that you have simultaneously developed a psychiatric illness called somatic symptom disorder? And there are even more 'illnesses' waiting in the wings. A category called 'Behavioral Addictions' may, in the future, include diagnoses like internet addiction disorder.

• Over two-thirds of members of the DSM-5 advisory task force have been shown to have links to pharmaceutical (drug) companies.[2] Since these companies have an obvious interest in increasing the number and range of diagnoses, this raises questions about the independence of the committee and its conclusions.

With the exception of a narrower set of criteria for autism spectrum disorder, the general effect of the *DSM-5* revisions is to create a massive expansion of psychiatric 'illness'. It has been calculated that the new diagnosis of binge eating disorder will create more than ten million new psychiatric 'patients', while disruptive mood dysregulation disorder will label millions of children as mentally ill. These changes lead to the increasing medicalisation of everyday life, in which normal reactions and problems are turned into 'illnesses' to be treated by medication.[3]

A particularly fascinating aspect of the debate is that some of the strongest concerns about diagnosis have been raised by the chairs of both the *DSM-III* committee, Professor Robert Spitzer, and the *DSM-IV* committee, Professor Allen Frances. Frances in particular has publicly criticised the way in which *DSM-IV* helped to create what he describes as three epidemics in the USA – a tripling of diagnoses of attention deficit hyperactivity disorder (ADHD), a twenty-fold increase in the diagnosis of autistic disorder, and most shocking of all, a forty-fold increase in paediatric bipolar illness (i.e., bipolar disorder in children). Because of his regret about these developments and the consequent overuse of powerful medications, sometimes on children as young as two, he has come out of retirement to campaign energetically to prevent *DSM-5* taking this process even further. He has an outspoken blog at www.psychologytoday.com and warns that '*DSM-5* will radically and recklessly expand the boundaries of psychiatry. Many millions will receive inaccurate diagnosis and inappropriate treatment'.[4]

As the date of publication of *DSM-5* approached in 2012, even more voices joined in. The British Psychological Society made an official comment on the proposed revisions to *DSM-5*:

Clients and the general public are negatively affected by the continued and continuous medicalisation of their natural and normal responses to their experiences; responses which undoubtedly have distressing consequences which demand helping responses, but which do not reflect illnesses so much as normal individual variation ...[5]

This was followed by an open letter and petition set up by the US Society for Humanistic Psychology calling for second thoughts about the revisions at www.ipetitions.com/petition/dsm5. It rapidly gathered support from over 15,000 individuals and 50 professional organisations.

But the most extraordinary events were yet to come. On the eve of publication, Thomas Insel, the director of the world's largest funding body for mental health research, the US-based National Institute of Mental Health (NIMH), dealt what was described as a body-blow to *DSM-5* by declaring that 'Patients ... deserve better ... The weakness is its lack of validity.' Moreover, he announced that NIMH would from now on be 're-orienting its research away from *DSM* categories'.[6] In other words, NIMH is calling for research to be based on experiences of distress that cut across diagnoses, such as hallucinations, low mood, confused thinking, or anxiety, not on 'schizophrenia' or 'bipolar disorder' and so on. Insel's predecessor, Dr Steven Hyman, described *DSM-5* as 'totally wrong, an absolute scientific nightmare'.[7] Allen Frances added that 'the *DSM-5* process has been secretive, closed and sloppy ... there is no reason to believe that *DSM-5* is safe or scientifically sound'.[8]

Faced with this onslaught of criticism, the chair of the *DSM-5* committee, Dr David Kupfer, did not have a very convincing defence. In fact he admitted:

> In the future, we hope to be able to identify disorders using biological and genetic markers that provide precise diagnoses that can be delivered with complete reliability and validity. Yet this promise, which we have anticipated since the 1970s, remains disappointingly distant. We've been telling patients for several decades that we are waiting for biomarkers [LJ: in other words, the discovery of evidence about the biological causes of schizophrenia and

so on, which would place diagnosis on a firm basis]. We're still waiting.[9]

Finally, the Division of Clinical Psychology, representing the UK's 10,000 clinical psychologists, issued an official statement about its position on psychiatric diagnosis. For the first time, a professional body has formally called for 'a paradigm shift in relation to the experiences that these diagnoses refer to, towards a conceptual system that is no longer based on a "disease" model'.[10] Translated into ordinary language, UK clinical psychologists are saying that psychiatric diagnosis is not fit for purpose, and we need to develop other, non-medical ways of describing and understanding mental distress.

What are the implications of this controversy?

It is important to note that critics of *DSM* and *ICD* are not necessarily opposed to the use of psychiatric diagnosis in principle, although they may be very worried about some of the *DSM-5* developments. Influential American psychiatrists like Frances, Insel, Hyman and Kupfer do not want the system abandoned. Rather, they are saying that although we don't have the evidence to support the current diagnostic categories as listed in *DSM* and *ICD*, we need to develop an improved version. In the meantime, their main defence is something along the lines of 'We know that *DSM* is deeply flawed, but we have to stick with it until we come up with something better – although the necessary research will take years, possibly decades'. This seems to contradict Allen Frances' unusually frank admission in one interview, 'There is no definition of a mental disorder. It's bullshit. I mean, you just can't define it.'[11]

Others agree with the Division of Clinical Psychology's position and argue that it is time to admit that we have reached the end of the road with this particular system.

We have failed to produce the evidence to support it, and moreover it has many damaging effects, such as stigma and discrimination. We have alternatives and we should be using them. Many service user organisations and campaigners, people with actual experience of being diagnosed, support this view. And of course there is a range of views in the middle – professionals, carers and service users who have found that diagnosis can be helpful, although nearly everyone thinks it is imperfect.

This is a long-standing debate, which goes back to the earliest days of psychiatry in the 19th century. There have always been critics who have argued that psychiatry's theories are flawed and its practices are damaging. What is new and surprising about this latest round of arguments is that the most devastating criticisms have come from within the heart of the psychiatric establishment, out of the mouths of the world's most senior and eminent psychiatrists – including the very people who were responsible for drawing up *DSM-III*, *IV* and *5*. If they themselves are agreeing with some of their fiercest opponents and admitting that psychiatric diagnosis really doesn't have any sound basis in research, where does that leave psychiatry? And where does it leave the users of psychiatric services?

Only time will give us the answer to the first question. However, it is significant that the journal published by the Royal College of Psychiatrists, the *British Journal of Psychiatry*, has recently published a series of articles on the theme that 'Urgent action is required to … ensure the future of psychiatry as a profession'.[12] If psychiatric diagnosis doesn't survive, many professions, but especially psychiatrists, will be faced with serious questions about their current roles.

The answer to the second question is, I believe, that it is time to offer service users a genuine choice about whether they want to accept a psychiatric label. This doesn't mean denying that they have difficulties; it doesn't mean that medication has no part to play; and it doesn't mean that we can always avoid taking people into hospital against their wishes, in extreme situations when they are a risk to themselves or others. However, in my view, it does mean that it is no longer scientifically, professionally or ethically justifiable to insist on psychiatric diagnosis as the only way of describing people's distress. If the authors of the diagnostic manuals are admitting that the diagnoses are not supported by evidence and that the process of developing them is 'not scientific', *then no one should be forced to accept them.* If many mental health workers are openly questioning diagnosis and saying we need a different and better system, *then service users and carers should be allowed to do so too.*

Patients are supposed to give informed consent to taking medication. In other words, they should be given an accurate picture of the advantages and drawbacks of anything that is prescribed for them, so that they can make a proper choice about whether to take it or not. If we apply the same idea to diagnosis, people need to be just as clear about the strengths and limitations of the evidence, and the advantages and disadvantages of thinking about their difficulties in this way. To do this, we need to take a closer look at exactly what a medical diagnosis is and does, and use this to highlight some of the flaws in the process of making a psychiatric diagnosis. The next chapter attempts this task.

Chapter 3
What are the problems with psychiatric diagnosis?

This chapter and the next one attempt to outline in accessible language some very complex issues. If you want to explore the subject in more depth, there is a list of suggested books and articles at the end of this chapter. These are written from a mostly critical perspective, as a counterbalance to the accounts that are typically given in patient information booklets, on mental health websites, in professional journals and in the media – so bear this in mind in your assessment of their arguments.

What are the problems with psychiatric diagnosis?

It may seem too obvious to be worth stating that if you give someone a psychiatric diagnosis, you are assuming that they are suffering from a *medical illness*. It follows from this that we expect them to adopt the role of *patient* and be *treated* mainly by *medication*, administered by *doctors* and *nurses* in *hospitals* and *clinics*. Psychiatric diagnoses are used unquestioningly not just in the mental health field, but almost everywhere else. The media talks about people with 'paranoid schizophrenia' who are said to be a risk to others. Soap operas try to educate the public about 'psychosis'. Celebrities disclose their histories of 'bipolar disorder'. Anti-stigma campaigns like 'Time to Change' urge us to be more tolerant towards people suffering from 'mental illness'.

In all these cases, it is assumed these labels are as accurate and straightforward as stating that people are suffering from cancer, or pneumonia, or arthritis, or heart disease. In fact these analogies are often used. People are told that they need to take their medication just like diabetics need to take insulin. The American Psychiatric Association has a public information video using the catch phrase 'Mental illness is an issue of chemistry not character'.[1] The Time to Change campaign uses the slogan 'As real as a broken arm'. Anti-stigma campaigns are based on hammering home the 'It's an illness like any other' message, in the hope that this will make mental distress more acceptable to the general public.

This way of looking at mental distress is sometimes referred to as the 'medical model' or 'biomedical model'. In brief, this is the idea that the various experiences people report – overwhelming anxiety, low mood, unpleasant voices, unusual beliefs and so on – are mainly caused by something going wrong in the brain or body.

Psychiatrists in the UK don't generally support what might be called a pure biomedical model, that is, the idea that your difficulties are *only* due to faulty genes, biochemical imbalances and so on, although this may be less true of their American counterparts. The currently popular version of the biomedical model is the 'biopsychosocial' or 'vulnerability–stress' model. As described in *A Straight Talking Introduction to the Causes of Mental Health Problems*,[2] this model assumes that people are born with some kind of vulnerability or predisposition to break down, which can be triggered by stresses such as poverty or bereavement. In other words, there is a mixture of causes, both what is going on in your brain (perhaps inherited) and what has happened in your life. If you are lucky, you will not just be prescribed medication, but will also be encouraged by professionals to pay attention to your social circumstances, your relationships and so on.

However there is a big problem that applies both to the pure biomedical model and to the vulnerability–stress or biopsychosocial version. This is that, as the chair of *DSM-5* admitted (Chapter 2, p. 14), there is no actual proof that breakdown is best understood as an 'illness' with biological factors as a cause, or even as a main contribution. There is no blood test or X-ray to tell if someone really is suffering from 'schizophrenia', 'bipolar disorder', 'personality disorder', 'ADHD', and so on. It is not widely appreciated that there is no solid evidence at all that any psychiatric problems (with the few exceptions that are discussed below) are the result of faulty genes, or biochemical imbalances, or any other identifiable cause in the body or brain.

This may seem hard to believe, given that we have all seen pictures of brain scans showing the difference between 'normal' and 'depressed' brains and so on. But it is no surprise that brains look different depending on what we are feeling. They also show characteristic patterns of activity if we are feeling happy, or sleepy, or alert, and we don't call these states 'illnesses' or 'brain disorders'. Our brains can also show lasting changes as a *result of* intense or long-term experiences – whether good (e.g., meditation) or bad (e.g., abuse.) Severe deprivation in early life leaves its mark on the brain,[3] as can the powerful drugs used to treat mental health problems. However, this is not a sign of a brain disorder of some kind: it is a result of the impact of the person's relationships and environment. Encouragingly, there is also evidence that psychotherapy – like all experiences – can help to reverse such changes.

It's important to be clear about the arguments here. Every human experience is reflected in our brains and bodies in some way, whether we are doing the washing-up, chatting to the neighbours, or watching TV. Similarly, every human experience depends to some extent on our genes – we can only watch TV because we are genetically coded to have eyes to see with, and we can only chat to the neighbours because we are programmed to develop language. But we don't see these activities as a sign of mental illness, despite the undoubted involvement of biology. Nor do we normally say that our brains or genes *cause* us to do these things, although they may *enable* us to do them.

In a very broad sense, then, a biopsychosocial model applies to everything we think, feel or do, but the narrower 'illness-triggered-by-stress' sense used in psychiatry has not been supported. To put it simply: not all human suffering is best understood as a disease process. On the contrary, there is very strong evidence that even the most severe forms of distress are the end result of a mixture of difficult life circumstances. I will return to this in Chapter 4, but in the meanwhile, these issues are discussed in more detail in *A Straight Talking Introduction to the Causes of Mental Health Problems.*[4]

The biopsychosocial or vulnerability–stress model is preferable to the narrow biomedical one, but in practice it can have equally serious faults. It can convey the message that the very traumatic events experienced by many service users are somehow not enough to explain their breakdown – they must have some genetic or biochemical flaw or else they would have coped. This is both untrue and insulting. The reasoning seems to be something like: 'No doubt it didn't help when X lost her job/was sexually assaulted by her neighbour/was bullied at school and so on, but we now need to get on and treat the underlying illness'. As a consequence, everything in the service user's life tends to be seen just as a 'trigger' for the 'illness'. The events will be recorded in the notes but possibly never addressed again, and in busy services, the result is that there may be very little attention paid to anything other than the medication. In the words of a former president of the

American Psychiatric Association, '… we have allowed the biopsychosocial model to become the bio-bio-bio model'.[5]

In summary, psychiatric diagnosis rests on very flimsy foundations, as do the biomedical and vulnerability–stress models that it supports.

What do we mean by medical diagnosis?

In order to explore this in more detail, it will be useful to think a bit more about the theory underpinning medical diagnosis. This is a complex subject, but essential to a full understanding of the criticisms and controversies.

What are the purposes of medical diagnosis?

A medical diagnosis serves a number of purposes. It helps us to decide on the correct treatment, predict the outcome (prognosis), provide a basis for research, suggest what the cause (aetiology) is, and enable professionals to communicate with each other. It also provides information and sometimes relief for patients and their carers, who will naturally want to know what the condition is, and it helps people to access services, benefits, support groups and so on.

However, diagnosis has another even more important function when it is used in psychiatry. It supports the idea that *psychiatry is a branch of medicine* – just like neurology, oncology, paediatrics and so on – in which the main cause of someone's difficulties is something that has gone wrong with the functioning of the body or brain.

Medicine is a branch of science, and every branch of science has to be based on a reliable way of describing and grouping together its basic elements. For example, in chemistry, we can group particular types of atoms together and this allows us to develop theories about the way that two chemical substances will react with each other. Over time, these research findings enable us to draw up general rules or laws about what we expect to happen, and we thus build up a body of scientific knowledge. Similarly, in medicine you need to be able to define different types of disease and distinguish them from each other. If you cannot come up with a clear definition of what we call 'cancer', based on research into changes in the body, you will not be able to work out whether someone is suffering from that disease rather than another one, or indeed whether they are perfectly healthy. That in turn will mean that you haven't got a solid basis for deciding on the best treatments, carrying out further research and so on. Not all medical diseases can be diagnosed reliably or easily in our current state of knowledge, but the general principles remain the same.

We can see that if we don't have a reliable classification system in psychiatry, whether it is *DSM* or *ICD*, this would be a serious problem in day-to-day practice. It would leave us with a series of fairly loose guesses about what type of 'mental illness' we are facing, how to distinguish it from a different type of mental illness and what treatment to use. It would also imply that psychiatry doesn't know a lot about what causes mental distress and therefore isn't very good at helping people to recover. In fact, it would mean that it is hard to draw the line between mental illness and sanity at all. Furthermore, it would be hard to fill the gaps by carrying out research, because we wouldn't have a sound starting point. For example, it would be hard to compare groups of people with and without certain 'mental illnesses' because we would have no definite way of deciding which group they should be in.

Some would argue that this is, in fact, exactly the state psychiatry is in. People typically collect a whole range of diagnoses as they progress through the system, and are often prescribed a whole range of different medications, on a basis that often seems like guesswork. We can now see how this situation comes about. If it seems like guesswork – well, that is pretty much what it is.

However, the implications of these arguments go further than this. The lack of a reliable and valid way of making diagnoses, in other words the lack of a proper classification system, raises very fundamental questions about whether psychiatry really is a science – and specifically, whether it should really be seen as a branch of *medicine*. In other words, we might be in the very strange position of admitting, as one psychiatrist has pointed out, that psychiatry is 'something very hard to justify or defend – a medical speciality that does not treat medical illnesses'.[6]

We can now appreciate why critics have made statements like: 'Diagnosis is the Holy Grail of psychiatry, and the key to its legitimation'.[7]

It is no wonder that the whole debate is so controversial. It is almost impossible to exaggerate the consequences of abandoning psychiatric diagnosis. Few people who have had experience of psychiatry – whether as professionals, researchers, drug company employees, service users or carers – would be untouched by such a dramatic shift, and many would face a profound change in their lives, careers and sense of identity.

Of course, in such a situation we would still be left with many very distressed and desperate people in urgent need of help. However, we might have to conclude that this help is not best delivered by psychiatry as it currently stands.

We will now examine these arguments more closely.

How are medical diagnoses made?

There is an important distinction in medicine between *symptoms* and *signs*. 'Symptoms' are the complaints which someone may take along to their GP or family doctor, such as thirst, tiredness, nausea, pain, dizziness and so on. Sometimes there is a change in the body such as a swelling or rash. Often, though, symptoms are quite subjective, and it is hard for others to confirm them. In addition, symptoms may have a great number of possible causes, which need to be narrowed down in order to work out what the underlying problem is.

For these reasons, a definite diagnosis depends on the doctor being able to identify underlying *signs*, such as blood cell counts, tissue samples, abnormalities that show up on X-rays and so on. This may be done by carrying out tests. The difference between signs and symptoms is that signs can be observed and confirmed by others. They can also be compared to an objective standard or 'norm', such as the expected cell count for a healthy person. The assumption is that there is some kind of biological mechanism associated with the sign and linking it with the symptoms.

To take an example, if someone presents with *symptoms* of thirst, tiredness and weight loss, diabetes might be suspected. The *sign* that would confirm this diagnosis would be the level of sugar in the urine, as shown in tests. This in turn is caused by poor reabsorption of glucose, which leads to the symptoms – tiredness, thirst and so on. Once the doctor has the test results, he or she can be confident that the patient's signs and symptoms match one particular pattern which has been established by medical research. At this point, a diagnosis can be confirmed or disconfirmed.[8] The doctor will be in a position to say, 'I'm afraid my initial guess based on what you told me was correct – you do have diabetes' or whatever. This is, of course, a simplification of a complex process, and in many cases our knowledge is still incomplete, but the general principles are clear.

At this point it is important to note that a small minority of psychiatric diagnoses do fit into this model. It seems clear that the various types of dementia, for example, are the result of changes in the brain which can be observed and confirmed with scans. The same is true of a minority of other conditions that are sometimes encountered on psychiatric wards, such as

Huntington's disease, a genetically transmitted neurological disease. These are definitely medical diseases. The causes of autism, a lifelong developmental disability, are not yet established, but are generally agreed to be biological in origin.

People can also have experiences which at first glance look like mental illness, but turn out on investigation to have biological causes. For example, older adults sometimes react to chest infections by developing highly unusual ideas or 'delusions'. These disappear when the underlying infection is treated by antibiotics.

However, the vast majority of psychiatric problems have no known biological causes. This includes conditions such as 'schizophrenia', 'bipolar disorder', 'clinical depression', 'personality disorder', 'paranoia', 'obsessive compulsive disorder' (OCD), 'anorexia nervosa' and 'ADHD'. It also includes 'psychosis' which is an umbrella term for people who have unusual beliefs and experiences.

In summary, making a diagnosis in other branches of medicine is firmly based both on research into the body and on a very large body of scientific knowledge about how it works and the various ways in which it can go wrong. Psychiatric diagnosis is, in some very important ways, a different process, as we will now discuss.

What are the differences between diagnosis in psychiatry and diagnosis in other branches of medicine?

We can illustrate this by looking at a list of some of the 'symptoms' that are said to make up schizophrenia, the condition that has been described as the 'heartland of psychiatry'.[9] (The *DSM-III-R* version is used here because it gives the most detailed description of the criteria,[10] although *DSM-5* is essentially the same.) As you read through the list, ignoring any unfamiliar jargon terms, you might want to make a mental note of what strikes you about these criteria.

Delusions

Prominent hallucinations

Incoherence or marked loosening of associations

Catatonic behaviour

Flat or grossly inappropriate affect

Bizarre delusions (i.e., involving a phenomenon that the person's culture would regard as totally implausible, e.g., thought broadcasting, being controlled by a dead person)

Prominent hallucinations of a voice with content having no apparent relation to depression or elation, or a voice keeping up a running commentary on the person's behaviour or thoughts, or two or more voices conversing with each other

Prodromal or residual symptoms (i.e., preceding or following the active phase):

- Marked social isolation or withdrawal
- Marked impairment in role functioning as wage-earner, student or home-maker
- Markedly peculiar behaviour (e.g., collecting garbage, talking to self in public, hoarding food)
- Marked impairment in personal hygiene and grooming
- Blunted or inappropriate affect
- Digressive, vague, over-elaborate or circumstantial speech
- Odd beliefs or magical thinking, influencing behaviour and inconsistent with cultural norms, e.g., superstitiousness, belief in clairvoyance, telepathy, and so on
- Unusual perceptual experiences, e.g., sensing the presence of a force or person not actually present
- Marked lack of initiative, interests or energy

The first thing you may have noticed is that these experiences are all at the 'symptom' level. As we have already said, there are no signs to confirm the presence of a psychiatric illness, which means that we are essentially left with a list of subjective reports. These experiences may be very real and distressing, but we can't actually link them to a biological 'sign', as we can with the signs of a physical illness, by using medical tests or investigations. It is a bit like grouping physical illnesses together on the basis that they all involve pain in your chest, or being out of breath, or having a headache. Obviously this would not get us very far since each of these complaints is likely to have a whole range of causes. Indeed they may not be a sign of illness at all (it is normal to be out of breath after exercise).

Since we don't have any signs to confirm the diagnosis, we can't actually tell if there is a biological disease process causing the experiences that we label as 'schizophrenia'. Nor can we tell the difference between, say, 'schizophrenia' and 'bipolar disorder' in the same way that in other branches of medicine we can use tests to work out whether someone is suffering from cancer or tuberculosis. In other words, the *DSM* and *ICD* committees have no way of checking whether the lists of criteria that they draw up – like the ones above – are actually sensible or meaningful clusters of 'symptoms'. They are just as likely to be a random set of experiences without a shared underlying cause. In contrast to the rest of medicine, the decision about what counts as 'schizophrenia' and so on is not based on research into the way the body works. In the end, it comes down to a vote by committee. New diagnoses are the end result of a process in which 'a few influential insiders decided that a new category would be clinically meaningful and handy and lobbied for its inclusion'.[11]

However, this is not the only difference between diagnosis in psychiatry and diagnosis in other branches of medicine. A more fundamental one is that the 'symptoms' listed in *ICD* and *DSM* are not actually complaints about the ways in which your body is functioning (pain, nausea, thirst, dizziness and so on). They are examples of unusual *thoughts, feelings and behaviours.*

This creates serious problems in working out where to draw the line between normality and abnormality – if, indeed, such a line can be drawn. It is relatively simple, in principle, to work out how the body ought to be working and to draw up standards in order to compare the results of tests; for example, investigating for tumours, or checking to see if someone's blood cell counts or enzyme levels fall within an acceptable range. But there is no way of measuring and getting universal agreement about standards for 'normal' ways of feeling, thinking and behaving, because such judgements depend both on a person's context (washing may be impossible if you are homeless) and on their culture (seeing visions may be 'normal' in some societies). There is no agreed definition of what a 'reasonable' level of initiative is, or how often you should have a bath. In fact, you may have noticed that every single one of the *DSM* 'symptoms' of schizophrenia involves making a subjective judgement of some sort. How flat does your affect (i.e., your emotional expression) have to be, and who decides this? How much food are you allowed to store before it becomes 'hoarding', and when do your beliefs turn into 'delusions'? At what point does your lack of hygiene become a medical symptom?

We can illustrate this further using the criteria for diagnosing 'personality disorder'. These are perhaps the most controversial diagnoses of all, since they are a judgement on you as a person, not just what you are experiencing. Your personality is not something you 'have', like a rash or a broken leg, or an experience you are going through, like hearing voices or feeling panicky – it is who you are. Moreover, this diagnosis carries implications of being both mad and bad. In fact, two psychiatrists have written that personality disorder is shorthand for 'the patients psychiatrists dislike … An enduring pejorative judgement, rather than a clinical diagnosis'.[12]

The most frequently diagnosed personality disorder, 'borderline personality disorder', appeared for the first time in *DSM-III* in 1980. It will probably not feature in *ICD-11*. Europeans who have been given this label can therefore look forward to abandoning it in about 2017.

Examples of the criteria for diagnosing personality disorder – the first from *DSM-IV* and the second from *ICD-10* – include:

Borderline personality disorder
A pattern of unstable and intense interpersonal relationships; markedly and persistently unstable self-image or sense of self; impulsivity in at least two areas that are potentially damaging, e.g., spending, eating disorders, reckless driving; inappropriate, intense anger.

Avoidant personality disorder
Belief that one is socially inept, personally unappealing, or inferior to others; excessive preoccupation with being criticized or rejected in social situations; unwillingness to become involved with people unless certain of being liked; avoidance of social or occupational activities that involve significant interpersonal contact because of fear of criticism, disapproval, or rejection.

These criteria raise the same questions as the ones for schizophrenia. They are lists of thoughts, feelings and behaviours, not bodily symptoms. Being impulsive and having intense and unstable relationships is not a disease, and nor is worrying about criticism or avoiding parties. We can all recognise individuals who fit the above descriptions, and some of them may have serious problems and be in need of help, but there are no objective standards to decide the cut-off with 'normality'. Indeed all of us, whether diagnosed as mentally ill or not, are likely to have some of these experiences at some time in our lives.

Moreover, if you added in the context behind the diagnosis you would be very likely to find a non-medical explanation for these behaviours. Maybe the young woman who is so distrustful in relationships has been sexually abused. Maybe the man who is terrified of social situations was severely bullied at school. All of these explanations would be more likely to lead to effective help than labelling people as having a 'disorder'.

The end result is that psychiatry is left with a series of circular arguments. Being given a psychiatric diagnosis sounds like an explanation – but in fact it isn't. The answer to 'Why do I hear hostile and critical voices?' is 'Because you have schizophrenia'. The answer to 'How do you know I have schizophrenia?' is 'Because you hear hostile and critical voices'. The same logic applies to every psychiatric diagnosis (with the exceptions already described). 'Why are my moods so up and down?' 'Because you have bipolar disorder.' 'How do you know I have bipolar disorder?' 'Because your moods are so up and down.' In other branches of medicine, there is an exit from this circle because we can run tests and identify underlying biological signs. ('Why am I getting such terrible headaches?' 'Because, as the scan shows, you have a brain tumour' and so on.) To date, psychiatry offers no such way out.

People sometimes say that they welcome a diagnosis because it gives them some kind of explanation. This is entirely understandable – everyone wants an explanation. My point is that psychiatric diagnosis does not actually explain anything. Moreover, as I will discuss later, there are much better explanations on offer.

More consequences of basing psychiatric classification on subjective judgements

So far, I have argued that distressing and confusing thoughts, feelings and behaviours are not the same as the bodily signs and symptoms of a physical disease process. Diagnosing mental illness therefore relies on subjective judgements about what is 'normal' in a particular context or culture. This is completely different from making a judgement about bodily functioning based on physical tests and established norms about how the body should work.

To summarise the argument: *Psychiatric diagnoses are based on social not medical judgements.* The language conceals this process – psychiatrists and other mental health professionals sound and act as if they are doing the same thing as doctors in other branches of medicine. In fact, they are doing something fundamentally different. They are making a series of judgements about how people ought to think, feel and behave.

This gives us further insight into why people with experience of psychiatry tend to collect a whole series of labels as they proceed through the mental health system. It is a consequence of the fact that there is no objective way of deciding which is the 'real' medical illness that you are suffering from – or indeed if you are suffering from a medical illness at all.

Reliability and validity

This brings us onto some slightly more technical issues, the *reliability* and *validity* of psychiatric classification. Any scientific classification system has to be able to demonstrate that it can achieve reasonable levels of reliability and validity, or else it is simply not fit for purpose.

'Reliability' describes the likelihood that when faced with the same patient and an agreed list of criteria, psychiatrists will come up with the same diagnosis. As one might expect from the arguments above, reliability in psychiatric diagnosis is extremely low. Even when measured in ideal circumstances where experienced clinicians are coached in the criteria and presented with patients who are thought to fit fairly neatly into one diagnostic group, they only agree on a broad diagnostic category about 50 per cent of the time.[13] In real-life clinical settings, faced with a more typical range of patients, reliability is even lower.[14] Another predictable problem is that many individuals will fit the criteria for more than one psychiatric disorder, and end up with several labels. This is known as co-morbidity.

One response to this 'fuzziness' of boundaries between diagnoses is to create what can be described as 'in between, just short of, and left over' categories.[15] 'Schizoaffective disorder' lies somewhere in between schizophrenia and depression. 'Dysthymia' applies to someone who is low in mood but just short of actual depression. Sub-categories with titles such as 'bipolar disorder not otherwise specified' and 'schizophrenia residual type' are used to sweep up any leftover cases. This does not increase reliability; instead, it suggests that the boundaries between different diagnoses have been artificially drawn up and do not accurately reflect any underlying biological patterns.

An even more important issue, if possible, is the *validity* of classification systems. There are different meanings of validity, but essentially it is about whether categories actually describe something in the real world. An example may help. In Biblical times, people were quite convinced that madness was caused by evil spirits. There were probably very high levels of agreement (reliability) about who was possessed by spirits. Nowadays scientists do not accept that evil spirits actually exist in the real world, invading people to drive them mad, even if their behaviour is highly disturbed. In other words, even a category that is used in a reliable way (everyone in the village agrees that this person is possessed by evil spirits) may not be a valid one.

If a category is not reliable, it cannot be valid. Establishing reliability is thus the essential first step – and as we have seen, this has not been satisfactorily achieved in psychiatric diagnosis. However, we also need to be aware that even if reliability has been established, validity does not necessarily follow.

Criticisms of the validity of psychiatric diagnosis have been made since the beginning of psychiatry. There was a great deal of debate in the 1960s in popular books by psychiatrists like RD Laing, Thomas Szasz and others.[16] These critics argued that 'mental illness' is a social, moral or value judgement, not a proper medical concept. In response, Laing was accused of blaming parents for their children's breakdowns. As I made clear in the introduction, I do not support a 'blaming' view of anyone. However, the main points made by these critics have never been satisfactorily answered – indeed, as we saw in Chapter 2, they have recently come to the surface yet again.

In summary the reliability and, even more importantly, the validity of psychiatric diagnosis are still very much open to question. In fact, as revealed in Chapter 2, some of the world's most senior psychiatrists have recently admitted that reliability and validity have not been achieved, and that what we are left with is, at best, a temporary and very flawed system which urgently needs to be replaced. Whether this will eventually happen through yet more biological research, or whether we need to look in a completely different direction, towards people's social contexts, life events and relationships, is very much disputed.

In the meantime, we face the disturbing possibility that diagnosing someone with 'schizophrenia' or 'bipolar disorder' or 'personality disorder' is actually no more scientific or evidence-based than saying that they have been possessed by evil spirits.

The cross-cultural context of psychiatric diagnosis

We can look at the same issues from a cross-cultural perspective. What are the limitations of using psychiatric diagnosis in different, mainly non-Western cultures? This is an important issue, given the growing movement to promote 'mental health literacy' – in other words, the acceptance of the Western psychiatric model of mental distress – across the globe.

The use of psychiatric diagnosis with minority ethnic groups and in other cultures shows very clearly that our subjective judgements about diagnosis are based on cultural norms. For example, Westerners might automatically assume that someone who regularly talks to his dead ancestors is 'mentally ill', and such a person might be at risk of being given a diagnosis of schizophrenia. This subjective judgement is based partly on the cultural beliefs of a particular Western society, although other cultures might see it differently.

One inevitable consequence is that people who do not come from the same white, Western culture as modern psychiatry does are more likely to be given a psychiatric diagnosis. This may partly explain the higher rates of diagnosis of schizophrenia in Afro-Caribbeans living in the UK.[17]

Diagnosis of genuine medical problems should work in the same way in different cultures. If you have cancer or diabetes in the UK or the US, then given the right medical tests, you should still be recognised as having those same illnesses wherever you are in the world. One of the oddest consequences of basing diagnosis on cultural norms is that you will, in effect, 'recover' as soon as you get off a plane in a country where your experiences are held to be 'normal', as might be the case for someone who hears voices or believes they can talk to the spirits of their ancestors.

There is a special section of *DSM* for so-called 'culture-bound disorders' which often sound exotic to Westerners, such as the diagnosis of 'windigo' in Algonquin Indians who develop a fear that they have been bewitched, or *taijin kyofusho* in Japan, in which sufferers have a deep fear of offending or hurting others. This section assumes that Western perspectives are 'truer' or less culturally influenced than non-Western ones – which is very much open to question. For example, the various types of eating distress are a largely Western phenomenon, and may seem just as bizarre from the perspective of some cultures as 'windigo' does to Europeans.

A more challenging argument is put forward by psychiatrists like Suman Fernando,[18] who argues that since all psychiatric diagnosis is ultimately based on Western values and assumptions, it simply cannot be applied or understood in non-Western cultures. Western medicine, for example, is based on the idea that mind and body can be studied separately, which is very different from traditional African, Asian and Native American worldviews. These cultures have no exact equivalent to our diagnostic practices, and may see what we would define as psychiatric disorders in religious, spiritual or ethical terms instead.

In summary, the exporting of Western psychiatric models across the world leads to 'undermining of existing cultural strategies for dealing with distress, more not less stigma for those with mental health problems, and the imposing of an individualistic approach that may marginalise family and community resources and divert attention from social justice'.[19] Writers like Ethan Watters have documented the chilling results of promoting Western values and beliefs, wrapped up in Western diagnostic categories, in other cultures.[20] Fernando argues that in doing this we are assuming that our worldview, in contrast to their more 'primitive' one, is superior and more 'true'. Fernando describes this as a form of 'psychiatric imperialism' which is more subtle, but no less damaging, than more obvious forms of colonialism.

More consequences of social judgement

So far, we have argued that in labelling people with a *disorder* or *illness*, we are actually making a value judgement based on social/cultural standards ('This is not the way we think people should run their lives in this society'). We are not, despite what the language of diagnosis implies, making a medical or scientific decision. If you look back at the DSM criteria on page 27 you can see that DSM actually admits this by using phrases such as 'bizarre beliefs … that the person's culture would regard as totally implausible' and 'odd beliefs … inconsistent with cultural norms' as criteria.

A particularly obvious example is the case of homosexuality, listed in *DSM-II* until 1974 when it became politically unacceptable to continue to describe it as a mental disorder. The controversy 'was not about research findings. It was a 20-year debate about beliefs and values.'[21] It was removed as part of the wider political campaign for civil rights for gay people. We can now appreciate that this was a clear case of a social judgement disguised as a medical one. Similarly, with the passing of time we can all recognise that it was ridiculous to diagnose 'drapetomania', or the 'irresistible urge to run away from plantations', in slaves in 19th-century America. Clearly, this allowed slave owners to maintain their position of power while describing protest as a sign of the slaves' 'mental illness'.

Similar issues arise in relation to the diagnosis of women. Feminists argue that the women who use psychiatric services can be understood as suffering from the pressures and contradictions of women's expected roles. For example, the enormous rise in eating disorders over the last 40 years, especially in women, is partly due to pressures placed on their appearance and weight, which are reinforced by multimillion pound diet, exercise and magazine industries. Women are also more frequently diagnosed with depression than men. It has been argued that this may reflect the fact that they are more likely to experience poverty and sexual abuse, along with inequality in jobs, pay, and so on, while carrying the major burden of childcare.

Women constitute 75 per cent of people diagnosed with 'borderline personality disorder'.[22] However, given the high incidence of sexual abuse in this group, there may be very good reasons for their anger, although this emotion is less acceptable in women. 'The diagnosis can be applied to women who fail to live up to their gender role because they express anger and aggression.' In fact it has been argued that 'fighting back is an appropriate response'.[23]

Summary

Once again, it is important to be clear about the argument. No one would deny that most of the people who use mental health services have severe problems. The question is whether 'diagnosing' these problems as being 'symptoms' of an 'illness' is a proper medical and scientific process, or simply a way of wrapping up our personal and social judgements about people's thoughts, feelings and behaviours in medical language. This raises serious questions about the whole practice of psychiatry as a branch of medicine.

Further reading on psychiatric diagnosis

Boyle, M (1999) Diagnosis. In C Newnes, G Holmes & C Dunn (eds) *This Is Madness: A critical look at psychiatry and the future of the mental health services* (pp 75–90). Ross-on-Wye: PCCS Books.

Bentall, RP (2003) *Madness Explained: Psychosis and human nature*. London: Penguin.

Caplan, P (1996) *They Say You're Crazy*. Philadelphia: Da Capo Press Inc.

http://www.dxsummit.org
This international website campaigns for and shares ideas about alternatives to diagnosis.

http://www.madinamerica.com/author/ljohnstone/
Blog on diagnosis and alternatives.

Johnstone, L (2008) Psychiatric diagnosis. In R Tummey & T Turner (eds) *Critical Issues in Mental Health* (pp 5–22). Basingstoke: Palgrave Macmillan.

Kinderman, P, Read, J, Moncrieff, J, & Bentall, RP (2013) Drop the language of disorder. *Evidence-Based Mental Health*, September 21, *16*, 2–3.

Kirk, SA & Kutchins, H (1997) *Making Us Crazy: DSM – The psychiatric bible and the creation of mental disorder*. New York, London: The Free Press.

Moncrieff, J (2010) Psychiatric diagnosis as a political device. *Social Theory and Health, 8*(4), 370–82.

Timimi, S (2011, 21 May) *No More Psychiatric Labels* http://www.criticalpsychiatry.net/?p=527

Many articles about the *DSM-5* controversy can be found at the very comprehensive website www.dxrevisionwatch.wordpress.com

Articles both for and against diagnosis as well as service user experiences can be found for free in *Journal of Mental Health*, 2010, *19*(4) http://informahealthcare.com/toc/jmh/19/4

What are the problems with psychiatric diagnosis?

Chapter 4
For and against psychiatric diagnosis in more detail

In the face of this crisis in psychiatry, numerous suggestions have been made about how to revise psychiatric diagnosis. Some have argued for a new name for schizophrenia, such as 'salience syndrome', and many professionals now replace the word 'schizophrenia' with the less-alarming general term 'psychosis' to include any experiences that are out of touch with reality. Although this may be preferable in some ways, it leads to even greater problems of reliability and validity, while still sounding like a medical diagnosis. To date, all the new ideas are all essentially modifications of the existing system, with the same drawbacks.

In the interests of promoting informed choice, I will briefly summarise a few more of the main arguments for and against the use of *DSM* and *ICD*. If this is too much detail for you, you may wish to skip forward to Chapter 5.

'We don't use DSM *in the UK, so these debates are irrelevant to us'*
In fact, as described earlier, *DSM* has a powerful worldwide influence because it is the preferred system for funding and publishing research. However, as also noted earlier, *ICD* is based on exactly the same principles as *DSM*. Both systems are about describing people's distress in terms of a medical diagnosis, and as such, both are open to the criticisms summarised in Chapter 3.

'Most psychiatrists and GPs hardly refer to DSM *or* ICD. *They work in a much more flexible way in actual practice'*

This is broadly true. At one level it is to be welcomed – making way for more common sense in psychiatry is always a good thing. At another level, it implies that on a day-to-day basis, diagnoses are being used in an even more unreliable way than officially admitted. This is also true. Different psychiatrists have their own preferences, which they often use without checking *DSM* or *ICD* criteria at all. Some apparently see a great many cases of borderline personality disorder, while others seem to be particularly good at detecting bipolar disorder. None of this increases confidence in the diagnostic system.

*'*DSM *and* ICD *don't claim to be lists of illnesses with medical causes. They are simply lists of descriptions which are a useful shorthand in our work'*

This is a very misleading argument. *ICD* is one chapter in a manual called the *International Classification of **Diseases*** (my emphasis). *DSM* and *ICD* use medical terms like 'illness', 'symptom' and so on. And in terms of the way that psychiatric diagnosis is actually used, few service users will have failed to receive the message that they are suffering from a medical illness – perhaps with causes like 'biochemical imbalances' – that is best treated by doctors and nurses, in hospitals, by medication. A list that really was just a neutral list of descriptions would be a very good starting point for helping people in distress, but *DSM* and *ICD* are not it.

'What about PTSD? That doesn't imply a biological cause'

Post-traumatic stress disorder is an unusual diagnosis because it is defined as being caused by something that has happened to you. Unfortunately the word 'disorder' still implies a kind of biological problem, rather than that you are having a normal reaction to an abnormal situation. Renaming it 'post-traumatic stress reaction' would provide us with a useful, non-medical, non-diagnostic description. We need more of that kind of category.

'How can you decide what treatment to have without a diagnosis?'

This question assumes that psychiatric diagnoses are reliable and valid, and do describe underlying medical illnesses. If this is not the case, then they will not be a helpful guide to what medication or other intervention to use. As Moncrieff argues in *A Straight Talking Introduction to Psychiatric Drugs*,[1] psychiatric medications do not cure diseases, or have specific effects on specific illnesses. In fact, the terms 'antidepressant', 'anti-psychotic', 'mood stabiliser' and so on are inaccurate and misleading. The drugs do not target 'psychosis', depression, mood swings and so on in the same way that antibiotics target infections. Instead, they have a range of general effects, such as sedation, on both 'normal' and 'abnormal' states of mind. These effects may sometimes be useful – for example, by helping you to feel less upset by hostile voices, or by reducing intense anxiety. But the drugs 'work' in the same way as alcohol does when it helps you feel more relaxed in social situations, and as Moncrieff asserts, 'No one suggests that alcohol works by reversing an underlying biochemical imbalance or correcting an insufficiency of alcohol in the brain.'[2]

The way that drugs are used in practice supports this. Neuroleptics ('anti-psychotics') have been recommended for schizophrenia, depression, anxiety, bipolar disorder, personality disorder and ADHD. Antidepressants have been recommended for a similarly wide range of problems, including borderline personality disorder, depression, obsessive compulsive disorder (OCD), anorexia, panic, social phobia and so on.[3]

Rejecting the diagnostic system doesn't mean rejecting the use of drugs. It simply means accepting the large amount of evidence that although they may help some people to cope, they are not the equivalent of antibiotics for infections, or chemotherapy for cancer, or insulin to help regulate blood sugar levels in diabetes. The service user should have the final decision about whether they are more helpful than harmful for him or her.

Similar arguments apply to decisions about what kind of psychological treatments to recommend. There are psychological therapies that may help with anxiety, or relationship difficulties, or flashbacks from trauma, or low mood, and so on, but these problems are found in a whole range of different diagnoses. The important thing is to be clear what kind of problem someone is experiencing. You don't have to use diagnosis to work this out. You simply need to be able to describe what their main problem is.

(Note: It is dangerous to stop taking any psychiatric drug abruptly. For more information on psychiatric medications and withdrawal, please see references at the end of the book. Discuss the options with your prescriber.)

'How can you carry out research without something as a starting point?'

It is true that you need some kind of name or definition as a basis for research, at least for the kind of study that is currently accepted as providing the strongest evidence. However, it is also true that if your starting point is neither reliable nor valid, your research efforts are not likely to get very far. In fact, this may account for the lack of findings after many decades of investigation into 'schizophrenia', 'bipolar disorder' and so on. This is why the prestigious National Institute of Mental Health announced that from now on it will be funding studies that are not based on diagnostic categories (see Chapter 2, p. 14). So, one answer to this question is to start with a simple description of a type of problem, not a diagnosis. In fact, one of the most productive areas of research in recent years has done exactly this. By using the neutral, non-medical term 'hearing voices' as a starting point, the Hearing Voices Network has produced findings that have dramatically changed our understanding of voice-hearing, and helped to develop a whole range of strategies to manage it.[4]

'The situation is similar in other branches of medicine'
It is true that matters are not always clear-cut in other branches of medicine. Many diagnoses such as fibromyalgia and chronic fatigue syndrome are at an early stage of development, and we are often unclear about the exact causes of conditions. Further research will clarify these questions, and show us whether these diagnoses need to be modified or perhaps abandoned as our knowledge increases. However, in general, the field of modern medicine is based on a large amount of well-established theory and evidence, which has led to the major advances of the last 50 years. The understanding and treatment of many types of cancer, for example, has been transformed. There has been no equivalent progress in psychiatry. In fact, some critics have argued that outcomes have actually got worse.[5]

It is also argued that diagnosis is often just as hard to make in other branches of medicine – for example in the case of multiple sclerosis. This may be true, but it is begging the question. No one doubts that multiple sclerosis is a neurological disorder, the result of something malfunctioning in the body (i.e., damage to the coating of the nerve fibres), even if it takes a while to confirm the diagnosis and even if the ultimate cause is still unknown. This is exactly the question that is yet to be answered in psychiatry: are these bodily illnesses at all?

'We do have the evidence that mental distress is a medical disease'

There is still a fair amount of simple assertion-by-experts around, such as 'Major advances in molecular biology and neuroscience over recent years have provided psychiatry with powerful tools that help to delineate the biological systems involved in psychopathology.'[6] Readers will have to make their own minds up about whether such statements can be justified, particularly given that several of the world's most eminent psychiatrists, as described in Chapter 2, are openly admitting that this is not the case. It is worth noting that even those researchers who are most firmly committed to this viewpoint have found that their genetic research does not map onto the current categories – or, as it has been phrased, 'DNA hasn't read *DSM*'. So, one way or another, whichever camp you come from, the current diagnostic system will need to be abandoned and rewritten from scratch. This is a strong argument for offering service users a choice about accepting these labels.

'We don't have the evidence that mental distress is a medical disease, but this is the best we've got until we come up with something else, so we need to stick with it for now'

As we noted in Chapter 2, this is the most common defence being put forward by psychiatrists at the heart of the controversy. British psychiatrist Simon Wessely said: 'A classification system is like a map. And just as any map is provisional, ready to be changed as the landscape changes, so is classification.'[7] But this depends on whether *DSM* and *ICD* do provide at least some guide to the territory. If they don't, then we are, quite simply, using the wrong map. To use an analogy, a map of Cornwall is of no help if you are driving round Scotland. You would be better off with no map at all than one which directs you down the wrong route. At the very least, you should be honest with service users about the limitations of the map, rather than insisting that they accept its geography and the consequences that follow.

This argument is usually followed by:

'We soon will have the evidence that mental distress is a medical disease'

According to some, psychiatry is just taking a while to catch up: 'If you went back 30 or 40 years in studying cancers or heart disease or whatever, you would also find that medicine wasn't at that stage ...'[8]

Millions of pounds and dollars continue to be invested in research projects that have failed to fill the gaps in psychiatric theory. But the harder we look, and the more sophisticated our investigations, the less we seem to find. The problem is that for some supporters, no evidence will ever be enough to show that mental distress is not a physical disease. In fact, this assumption is not stated in terms that can be disproved. It is an article of faith, not a proper scientific hypothesis, and as soon as one theory collapses (e.g., 'Perhaps it is a biochemical imbalance of some kind'), supporters simply grasp at another one, and so the game continues. The new favourite is abnormalities of brain circuits (groups of brain cells). Should we continue to throw more money in the same direction, or should we re-direct it towards addressing some of the many psychological and social factors that are known to increase the risk of mental distress?

One final argument deserves consideration.

'But surely you have to categorise things somehow?'
This is a valid and interesting point. We have an innate need
to categorise; human beings learn to group things together
from the moment they are born (mother versus stranger,
and so on). In the same way, we need to be able to group
various experiences of distress together in order to fulfil all
the purposes of diagnosis discussed so far – working out what
may have caused it, how best to help, and so on. But whether
or not the particular type of categorisation known as diagnosis
is useful is another question.

Recent research has begun to suggest some alternative
ways of grouping mental health problems together. We now
have an overwhelming amount of evidence for factors that
are known to make it more likely that people will break
down. There is no room for a detailed discussion here, but
they are summarised in *A Straight Talking Introduction to
the Causes of Mental Health Problems.*[9] Briefly, these causal
factors tend to divide into two main groups. The first group
is social circumstances. This includes poverty, discrimination,
unemployment, poor housing, loneliness and isolation, and
so on. The second group is relationship factors. This includes
domestic violence, rape, sexual, physical or emotional abuse
in childhood, bullying and other forms of victimisation, loss
and bereavement, and so on. We already know a lot about the
possible effects of these events, and we are starting to learn
more. For example, until recently it was not appreciated that
sexual abuse can increase the likelihood of hearing hostile
voices, or that bullying and victimisation can make it more
likely that you will later develop 'paranoid' ideas.

We cannot and probably never will be able to make
neat links between particular kinds of events and particular
mental health difficulties. For example, it seems as if
childhood adversity increases the risk of *all* types of mental
health problem, from low mood and eating disorders to

'psychosis'.[10] It is also clear that not everyone who is abused will suffer long-term effects, and conversely, not everyone who seeks psychiatric help has experienced obvious forms of trauma and deprivation. As we will discuss, each person's story is different. However, we do know enough to be able to start thinking in general terms that are not based on psychiatric diagnosis (as many therapists have always done). Instead of reaching for a label, we can be discussing with the service user: 'Is this a response to a trauma of some kind? Or is this a reaction to your struggles as a lone parent? Or is it about a series of losses that you have never really grieved for?' and so on.

There is nothing wrong with searching for patterns in experiences of distress – indeed, it is essential. The problem arises when we impose a *preconceived* classification system which does not account for people's actual lived experiences and, moreover, does not even fit the evidence.

Summary

We have now spent quite a while discussing complex theoretical issues. While this probably hasn't been the easiest read, we will have a better understanding of how psychiatric diagnosis works (or doesn't work) in practice if we have a grasp of the underlying theory and its strengths and limitations.

The simplest answer to the question of 'What do we do instead of diagnosing people?' is 'Stop diagnosing people'. The argument that we need a fully worked-out alternative system before we can abandon something that is admitted to be non-valid even by the people who invented it is, in my view, a complete red herring. And the simplest current alternative is to *ask people what their problems are*, and start from there. Your problem might be that you have huge mood swings, or hear terrifying voices, or are too scared to leave the house, or feel suicidal, or can't stop cleaning and checking. There is a great deal of research on psychological and self-help approaches to all of these problems. Perhaps coupled with medication to take the edge off the worst distress, we already have the information to work out what might be helpful for a particular individual. Other alternatives will be discussed in Chapters 7 and 8.

Before we get there, it is time to look more closely at the impact of psychiatric diagnosis on the day-to-day practice of psychiatry. Following that, we will discuss the actual lived experience of receiving such a diagnosis.

Chapter 5
The wider impact of psychiatric diagnosis

The effects of psychiatric diagnosis in services

One of the main purposes of diagnosis is, as discussed earlier, to enable people to get the help they need within services. A diagnosis is the essential gateway to accessing this. Mental health services vary, like any others, but I know from personal experience that the vast majority of staff are caring and dedicated people and that many service users are greatly helped and supported by their contact with psychiatry. Unfortunately this is not always the case. I believe that psychiatric diagnosis plays a key role in creating the situation where, despite everyone's best intentions, service users may end up feeling unheard, unhelped and even re-traumatised. This can happen in various ways:

The sick role
There are common messages or understandings about what it means to be diagnosed as being ill in Western culture.[1] It is worth spelling these out, because they often have an unhelpful influence in psychiatry.

When a doctor officially confirms that you have an illness by giving you a diagnosis, this is generally taken to mean that you are not responsible for your condition, and that you need to rely on expert help to get better. For example, we do not blame people for getting cancer and nor do we expect them to cure themselves; they need to follow medical advice. As we have seen, this is one of the reasons that people sometimes welcome a psychiatric diagnosis – it seems to let them off the hook of blame, guilt and responsibility and offer the hope of an expert solution. However, these messages do not fit so well in psychiatry. As any honest psychiatrist will admit, there are no medical cures for 'schizophrenia', 'depression', 'psychosis' and so on. The most that medication can do – and of course this can be life-saving at times – is to take the edge off the worst feelings.

So, it is not helpful for people going through a mental health crisis to be encouraged to hand over responsibility for their recovery to the professionals, and wait for the pills to cure them. Inevitably, the medical cure fails to materialise and the people in distress lose hope. Meanwhile, professionals quickly become frustrated with people who seem to be sitting around and not helping themselves. Service users are initially seen as having no responsibility (because they cannot help being 'ill'), but then there is a gradual switch towards seeing them as having complete responsibility for their feelings and behaviour; they are 'unmotivated' or 'attention-seeking' or 'don't really want to get better'. Even more damningly, they may be told they are 'treatment-resistant', with implications of both hopelessness and blame.

These mixed messages about responsibility keep everyone stuck. They can be summarised as: 'You have an illness which is not your fault *BUT* you retain responsibility for it and must make an effort to get better *BUT* you must do it our way because we are the experts in your illness.' It is almost impossible for service users to get things right. Either they are 'non-compliant' – not taking their meds as prescribed – or they are 'too dependent' – wanting more support than professionals are prepared to offer. Either they reject their diagnosis through 'lack of insight' or they become too attached to it and hang around on the ward being 'unmotivated'. Either they are too demanding of services, in which case they run the risk of being diagnosed with borderline personality disorder and sent away, or they refuse to engage with services, in which case an Assertive Outreach team may arrive on their doorstop and try to coerce them into some unwanted form of activity or treatment. These confusions are the inevitable result of applying a medical model to non-medical problems. Muddled thinking leads to muddled practice, and both staff and service users become stuck, frustrated and demoralised in the resulting contradictions.

As we noted in Chapter 1, we need a much more sophisticated position which acknowledges that people are in extreme distress and struggling to find a way forward *and* are responsible, capable people with many strengths who can, with the right support, start to take control of their lives again. This will be extremely difficult as long as we continue to use psychiatric diagnosis.

The treatment barrier
Another destructive consequence of psychiatric diagnosis has been called the 'treatment barrier'.[2] The message of psychiatric diagnosis, like medical diagnosis in general, is that the difficulties have arisen within the individual. In fact, nearly all psychiatric breakdowns arise partly as a result of relationship difficulties. Let's take the example of domestic violence. A woman who feels trapped in an abusive relationship is very likely to feel low, anxious and desperate. However, diagnosing her as having a mental illness called 'clinical depression' or 'bipolar disorder' locates all the problems within her – or perhaps within her brain chemistry. This makes it much harder for her to find her way out of the trap. She may be confirmed in her belief that there's something wrong with her and everything is her fault, and her partner may have an extra

excuse for his abusive behaviour. The real reasons for her low mood become sealed off behind a 'treatment barrier', as she takes on the role of psychiatric patient.

The messages of diagnosis can undermine alternative approaches. Honos-Webb and Leitner have explored how a diagnosis hinders therapy by feeding into people's negative beliefs about themselves, leading to a sense of despair that takes a long time to undo.[3] Recent research suggests that people who are given the 'chemical imbalance' theory of depression are more pessimistic about recovery and have less faith in therapy.[4] Moreover, even if the people themselves are able to see themselves differently, this may not be welcomed by others. In the example above, an abusive partner may be quick to tell the woman she is getting 'ill' again if she becomes more assertive. In this way, a diagnosis can make it harder for people to make changes in their relationships.

Loss of personal meaning

Perhaps the most damaging consequence of diagnosis, underpinning all the other factors, is the loss of personal meaning. If hearing voices, or being low in mood, or intensely anxious, or fearing that you are being poisoned by your relatives are diagnosed as the 'symptoms' of an 'illness', there is no more reason for professionals to explore their meaning than to ask about the meaning of a rash, or the content of delirious speech in a fever. As a result, people can spend years coming in and out of hospital without anyone sitting down and discussing their experiences and their distress in order to make sense of them. This is one of the commonest complaints made by service users, as Peter Beresford notes in *A Straight Talking Introduction to Being a Mental Health Service User*: 'Nobody's interested in you and you need so much to talk to someone and … just that opportunity was never given to me'.[5]

Stopping people from telling their stories

It may seem extraordinary that people's life stories are routinely unheard in psychiatric settings. I have often puzzled over this myself. I can recall numerous occasions when, after ten minutes, talk and a simple enquiry about what has happened in someone's life, a whole hidden story spilled out which made the person's feelings and experiences entirely understandable. It is as if diagnosis and the biomedical model have blindfolded staff from seeing what is in front of their very eyes.

Research into the way staff and patients relate in psychiatric settings shows how psychiatrists may actively select information that fits the psychiatric view, while discouraging people's attempts to talk about their experiences in other ways. A close examination of 32 interviews between people diagnosed with psychosis showed their psychiatrists structuring the conversation with a series of questions about mood, sleep, appetite and so on. The service users' frequent attempts to discuss their experiences were met with reluctance, avoidance and discomfort.[6] As a consequence, service users seem to 'self-select from the range of their experiences only those that are relevant to a psychiatric examination'.[7] The whole process is reinforced by actions of the rest of the staff on a daily basis.[8] And it is all written up in the notes as if it was an objective record of facts about the person, rather than a medical story that was actively (although not necessarily consciously) created by the most powerful participants.

The same process has been described in professional meetings, where the struggle for whose model of distress will win, the biological one or the psychological and social one, is played out in ward rounds and team meetings.[9] I can confirm that this happens on a daily basis in psychiatric settings. Like service users, staff may be very frustrated about it but feel powerless to change it. One team member said: 'I think it's really damaging. I think it's really awful. I mean you know you put that diagnosis of paranoid schizophrenia, of borderline personality disorder, of manic depression on someone, they've got it for life, end of story.'[10] However, team members who speak out may find their views discounted in various ways; for example, accusations of 'dividing the team', having 'extreme' views and so on.[11] Even if service users do raise the subject of abuse and trauma, they may not be believed: 'The horrendous abuse which I had disclosed "never happened" – even thinking it did was part of my illness. If the abuse did happen (one psychiatrist did believe me) then, in his words, "Pandora's box should never have been opened".'[12]

The social impact of psychiatric diagnosis

Stigma and discrimination

Whatever your view about the validity of psychiatric diagnosis, it is universally acknowledged that these labels lead to stigma and discrimination. A recent survey found that nearly nine out of ten people with mental health problems report being misunderstood by family members, shunned and ignored by friends, work colleagues and health professionals, or called names by neighbours. The effect was to prevent them taking part in everyday activities such as shopping, visiting the local pub, going on holiday, accessing educational opportunities, and applying for jobs. People from black and ethnic minority backgrounds, and people with disabilities, reported particularly high levels of discrimination.[13]

There has been a whole series of campaigns in the UK to combat stigma, including the Royal College of Psychiatrists' 'Changing Minds: Every family in the land'[14] and 'Defeat Depression'. The biggest and most recent one, 'Time to Change', has been running since 2007. All of them are based on the 'illness like any other' model. This is an uphill task, given that surveys show that the majority of the public, all over the world (including service users and carers) tend to see mental health problems as understandable responses to life events and circumstances.[15]

Unfortunately, there is a considerable amount of evidence that the 'illness' model does not reduce stigma but, particularly in the case of more serious conditions like 'schizophrenia', increases it. In fact people who believe that mental distress is a kind of biological illness are more likely to see psychiatric patients as dangerous and unpredictable.[16] While they may be less inclined to blame patients for their behaviour, at the same time they are more likely to fear and wish to avoid them.[17] The very act of labelling behaviours or feelings as 'mental illness' or 'schizophrenia' etc. increases rejection and desire for distance, largely by increasing perceptions of dangerousness, unpredictability, difference, and pessimism about recovery.[18] This is not surprising given that the message of these campaigns, however well-meaning, is that people with psychiatric problems are fundamentally different at a genetic or biological level.

There is an important distinction to be made between stigma and discrimination. Stigma is a person's internal sense of shame, inadequacy and difference, while discrimination refers to the unfair and oppressive barriers to full participation in society, such as being taunted or threatened in public or turned down for jobs. Recently, dramatic cuts to the welfare system, and the introduction of enormously stressful procedures for accessing benefits, have greatly increased the pressure on service users. Time to Change, which is partly funded by the UK Department of Health, has been entirely silent about these issues.

The debate about diagnosis suggests three alternative strategies that might be more likely to relieve the terrible burden of shame and exclusion blighting the lives of people with mental health problems; first, making the main focus of the campaigns on discrimination, social justice and fair access to welfare support; second, dropping the language of diagnosis which creates so much of the problem in the first place; and third, promoting the message that mental distress is not an 'illness like any other' but an understandable response to overwhelming life circumstances.

Summary

The argument of the last two chapters is that although there are some positive aspects to psychiatric diagnosis, there are also many negative ones, both at an individual and at a service and societal level. If you think psychiatric diagnosis should be retained, then your main concern will be to reduce some of these damaging consequences by, for example, education about mental health problems and anti-stigma campaigns. If you do not believe that psychiatric diagnosis is valid in the first place, this is additional confirmation that it is time for a fundamental change in the way we describe mental distress. Or you may take a middle position: perhaps you are unsure or unconcerned about diagnosis as a whole system, but you do believe that it is/isn't helpful for you personally.

Replacing a whole system that depends on diagnosis is, of course, a huge task that will take years. However, professionals should always remember that giving someone a psychiatric diagnosis is an immensely powerful act which has profound implications for their identity, relationships, place in the community, employment, health and future.

For all these reasons, some people have made the decision that at a personal level, they will no longer choose to define themselves or their difficulties in this way. While they may still have many struggles in their lives, they will no longer identify themselves as 'bipolar', 'personality disordered', 'schizophrenic', or 'mentally ill'. Many of them see this as a turning point in their recovery. Some of these stories will be explored in Chapter 8.

Chapter 6
The personal impact of psychiatric diagnosis

Whether or not we see psychiatric diagnosis as valid, we know that it is very powerful, and has a major impact on someone's life. For this reason it is very important that whatever our views, we listen to service users' accounts of the actual experience of being psychiatrically diagnosed.

Surprisingly, there is not a great deal of research into the impact of receiving a psychiatric diagnosis. The quotes below are drawn from personal accounts as well as journal articles. I have tried to make this a fair representation of the literature.

Trying to make sense of the implications of a psychiatric diagnosis is an active and ongoing struggle for most people, and they are likely to have mixed feelings about it, rather than one simple view. They may also change their views over time. Some diagnoses (schizophrenia, personality disorder) are more stigmatising than others (obsessive compulsive disorder (OCD), depression, anxiety disorder, attention deficit hyperactivity disorder (ADHD) etc.) and may therefore lead to stronger reactions. The quotes in this chapter mainly apply to people who were given diagnoses at the more severe end of the spectrum, although all psychiatric labels have the potential to lead to similar reactions.

Positive reactions

Relief at knowing 'what is wrong'

> *I had something that I could firmly grasp, and, you know, I could find out more and try to resolve it ... [I] felt relief that this whole jungle was going to be sorted out.[1]*

> *It gave me the comfort of explanation ... When I was told that I was depressed it gave me a framework of understanding and a first grip on what was happening.[2]*

Hope for treatment

> *Illness meant treatment and the possibility of cure.[3]*

> *Acceptance of my illness was a turning point ... By accepting treatment I could actively seek the right medication, access support, and turn my life around.[4]*

Having your distress recognised

> *My label initially brought comfort and validation for my struggles. It also ensured that I was given meds – some of which I desperately needed at the time.[5]*

> *So [psychiatrist] interviewed me and said that I had bipolar which I can see now with my money problems and the way I've sort of behaved in the past. Definitely not normal.[6]*

Freedom from blame and guilt

> *Diagnosis implied that this was an illness and not my fault – important for someone whose depression has always been riddled with guilt.[7]*

> *It's [a diagnosis of bipolar disorder] taking a bit of the guilt away that I feel for all the things that have happened, that I've done ...*[8]

A route to information and support

> *I chatted to quite a few people, a lot of people, with that diagnosis and it kind of helped because you could be so open about it and it was such a relief to be able to say, you know what, this happens to me and recognising that ... everyone kind of experiences similar things and it's quite comforting to know.*[9]

> *I think I prefer my illness having a name because it makes me feel less lonely, and I know that there are other people experiencing my kind of misery.*[10]

Commentary

In our current system, very few service users are able to avoid diagnosis altogether. Whatever their personal viewpoint, most will have to accept a diagnosis of some kind, at least nominally, in order to access essential services, benefits and so on. This is even more true in the US where insurance payment depends on having an official label. That is how the system works at present.

Everyone needs a way of understanding their painful experiences. As psychologist Gail Hornstein has written: 'There is no question that people will use the diagnostic categories and symptom criteria of the *DSM* to make sense of their feelings, thoughts and actions if they have no alternative: some explanation is always preferable to none at all.' This accounts for the relief at 'knowing what it is'.[11] However, we should bear in mind that this relief assumes that the diagnosis itself is valid. If it isn't, you are simply being offered a circular explanation of the kind described in Chapter 3: 'Why are my moods so up and down?' 'Because you have bipolar disorder.' 'How do you know I have bipolar disorder?' 'Because your moods are so up and down.'

In addition, if relief is based on the belief that the naming of the condition will lead to a simple and effective medical treatment, the service user is likely to be disappointed. As already discussed, there are no medical cures for psychiatric difficulties. Some of the above quotes come from people who later came to see their diagnoses as very unhelpful, and rejected them.

In these responses, we can see the effect of the 'brain or blame' dilemma – as if being given a diagnosis is the only way of escaping from a crippling sense of guilt. Nevertheless, for these people, diagnosis did represent relief, validation of their feelings, and hope for recovery. In Chapter 7 we will discuss whether there are other, non-diagnostic ways of conveying these messages and conferring these benefits which have a greater claim to be valid or in some sense 'true', and which have fewer of the negative aspects described below.

Confusion and lack of understanding

Some people's reactions were neither positive nor negative, but simply conveyed a sense of confusion about the number of diagnoses they were given and what they meant.

I was labelled with all sorts: eating disorder not otherwise specified, major depressive disorder, borderline personality disorder, schizoaffective disorder and eventually schizophrenia.[12]

In one week I had two appointments and on the Tuesday they told me that I had manic depression, and on the Thursday they told me it was schizophrenia. What do you do with that? ... I can't even spell schizophrenia so what are you supposed to do with these bizarre diagnoses?[13]

To try and find out more about it ... it was almost as though I had to be quite challenging to professionals ... by being persistent, and for quite a large part of the response in that was ... I'd be put under the hat of being a difficult client.[14]

Commentary

Lack of explanation of what the diagnosis means is commonly reported – indeed, service users are often not told what it is: 'Not once has a clinician given a diagnosis directly to me.'[15] This appears to be particularly common in the case of the more stigmatising diagnoses such as 'borderline personality disorder'. People are then even more confused, and open to all kinds of fears and misunderstandings.

Mixed reactions

My affective reactions to these various diagnostic terms have included puzzlement, relief, recognition, anger, curiosity, reassurance and alienation (often several at once), and they have varied significantly over a number of years.[16]

For a number of years, I accepted the medical model as a framework of understanding ... But I gradually came to appreciate drawbacks to the framework. My reading suggested the model might not stand up scientifically ... By the time I was entering my second decade of service use, the medical model, which I had initially found reassuring, seemed increasingly unsatisfactory, without the capacity to encompass the complexity of my interior or exterior life and give it positive value. As a result, I began to actively explore frameworks that better met my needs.[17]

Commentary

Commonly, people find that diagnosis has both positive and negative impacts. A survey of people diagnosed with 'psychosis' found that it was both a means of access to treatment and support, and at the same time a cause of disempowerment through messages about hopelessness and so on. Diagnosis helped by naming the problem and relieving people from self-blame, but hindered them by labelling them as a person and leading to stigma and discrimination.[18]

People may also find that although the diagnosis is of some help at first, they later wish to move on from it. This suggests another option for service users: accepting your diagnosis initially, but deciding at some future point that you wish to 'unlabel' yourself and free yourself from its less helpful messages.

Negative reactions

Loss of sense of self and identity

> Oh my God, I have no idea who I am anymore![19]

> I walked into [the psychiatrist's office] as Don and walked out a schizophrenic … I remember feeling afraid, demoralised, evil.[20]

> With the snap of a finger, I was labeled and forever changed. I was now a case in a file, a category, a collection of symptoms. I walked out with a script in my hand, not sure of what had just happened.[21]

The end of your life as you have known it

> The word 'schizophrenia' was momentous enough to account for the cataclysmic tremors I experienced inside. It

rang in my ears, a death toll for the life I had once known. [22]

Life as I now knew it had just completely ended. [23]

Feeling different, labelled and stigmatised

I'll never be able to erase the ink that's been put on me. [24]

I already knew something was wrong with me. Now I knew I was mad ... The diagnosis becomes a burden ... you are an outcast in society ... It took me years to feel OK about myself again. [25]

I've always adopted a policy of telling people; you know, they'll find out. 'Cos we are different. [26]

Part of society sees schizophrenics as dangerous and unacceptable. I have had it from my parents, my family and my friends. [27]

Stigma and the family

Growing up with a mentally ill mother was oppressive and worrisome ... I was terrified that I was like my mother and therefore had something wrong with me. Acutely self-conscious, I felt inferior to other children. [28]

Our relationship with the church faltered. The church was not there for parents of a mentally ill child. It seemed that the minister couldn't even talk about mental illness. [29]

My family has been shamed and defamed by psychiatric diagnosis. Our lives, historical and present, are forever affected by it. We have felt different. We have felt defective and unacceptable. We felt that our genes were

*inadequate and shouldn't be reproduced. We felt that our
diagnoses had to be hidden because others might think us
dangerous or unpredictable. At times, we felt so 'other'
that we had to hide our experiences even from one another.
We lived with secrets and silence that reached into every
corner of our lives ...[30]*

Hopelessness and despair

*My diagnostic label promoted despair and threatened to
become a self-fulfilling prophecy.[31]*

*I don't know that you have much of a future with this
illness.[32]*

*I have been diagnosed with dysthymic disorder since I
was thirteen. One kind of harm I suffered from receiving
a diagnosis, in and of itself, was that it seemed so final
and despairing to receive as a teenager. For me, having a
diagnosis seemed so final. Like it wasn't just a temporary
issue that I was having, adjustment or adolescence or
something, but this disorder that I was going to have for
the rest of my life no matter what I did.[33]*

Shame and humiliation

*Being diagnosed as schizophrenic was deeply humiliating
... [it] taught me to distrust my innermost feelings and
thoughts, and encouraged me to surrender my autonomy
and self-reliance to others. It pushed me deeper into
isolation and separation from the rest of humanity.[34]*

*I had to learn to hide and deny who I was as a human being
and often hide certain things from different people so that
they would not be used against me.[35]*

Fear, inadequacy and self-blame

If I could make one statement about what the diagnosis does to hurt me, I would say 'It causes me to live in fear and never feel like I am good enough no matter what I do in life no matter how good it is'. Even if no one else knows that I have these labels, I do, and I have lived my life trying to be perfect, knowing that was impossible for anyone but beating myself up when I failed to be.[36]

But the worst part of this, which I have only been recently able to shake within the last year ... is the defectiveness I felt. Just kind of in some core way. Like I'm totally different.[37]

Social isolation

I needed to be able to relate to other people what I felt – why I felt so stigmatised by my illness that I couldn't relate to anybody. I felt very alone and very lonely.[38]

I lost all of my friends ... yes I lost them all ... It was just being in hospital and then when I did come out of hospital they would taunt me ... I had side-effects from shaking, like this, and you know they would taunt me about, you know. I just lost all my friends with being in hospital.[39]

Discrimination

We're not accepted when we go back to work, no matter that you do the job ... They don't treat you as an equal, they're always a bit wary of you.[40]

I went for a job just recently at a local bakery and I saw a lady there who interviewed me. And as soon as I mentioned – I put it as nicely as I could – that I had had a nervous breakdown ... her face dropped and her attitude completely changed. I could tell it wasn't my imagination and of course I get the letter in the post a few days later saying 'Thanks, but no thanks'.[41]

The diagnosis of 'personality disorder'

As discussed in Chapter 3, the diagnosis of personality disorder seems to be experienced particularly damagingly because of its implications of badness as well as madness, and the message that because this is who you are, you may never recover. With only a few exceptions, people's reactions to being given this label seem to be overwhelmingly negative.

I was so offended. I was really offended. I thought well, 'F∗∗∗ you!' You're attacking my personality; you're attacking me. You're attacking the very soul of me, you know; who I am, and what I am, that's a disorder.[42]

For a long time I was told it was untreatable, which didn't help my outlook on things at the time.[43]

The killing of hope ... it almost feels like, well, your hands are tied, your cards laid and your fate set.[44]

It was a dustbin label ... it was just a diagnosis where you don't fit into other categories.[45]

As a group we already feel sub-human, misunderstood and vulnerable, and now we are tarred with the brush of being bad as well as mad.[46]

It [a diagnosis of BPD] makes it sound like it's my fault, it's my personality ... [like] I was born wrong so it was never going to be good.[47]

Summary

The quotes in this chapter show how diagnosis can represent, in the words of one researcher, both 'salvation and damnation'.[48] It is understandable that service users, reaching desperately for an escape from anguish, confusion, guilt and blame, might see diagnosis (at least initially) as 'salvation'. However, these benefits may be bought at the high price of taking on profoundly destructive messages of defect, dangerousness, damage and despair.

Once accepted, these labels are extremely 'sticky'. Recovery from a physical illness means being able to leave that identity behind you. With luck and the right treatment, you will no longer be, for example, an appendicitis patient and no one will see you in those terms any more once you leave hospital and recover. The shadow of psychiatric breakdown does not disappear so easily, if at all – partly because people are often told it is a lifelong condition. Moreover it tends by its nature to define you as a person, not just as someone who has a particular problem.

People who are given a psychiatric diagnosis are, almost by definition, likely to be carrying feelings of shame, worthlessness, failure and hopelessness. Official confirmation that you are fundamentally flawed and different from others strongly reinforces these feelings, and at the same time makes it harder to challenge the expert verdict. The diagnosis can also become a self-fulfilling prophecy. Told that you can't be reliable/responsible/accountable because of your illness, you stop being responsible/accountable/reliable, which becomes further confirmation of your disability, and so on. It is very hard to extricate yourself from these vicious circles.

These quotes raise the important question of how much of the suffering and hopelessness of 'mental illness' is due to the original problems, and how much is created by the process of psychiatric diagnosis itself.

Concluding thoughts

Despite evidence of the damaging effects of the process of diagnosis, resisting it is not easy:

> *I fought with all my might to prevent the vocabulary of mental illness from becoming second nature to me. I refused to accept that what I was experiencing was symptomatic of bipolar disorder. Depression, maybe, but bipolar disorder, most surely not. This diagnosis and the resulting requirement that I take medications fueled my anger more. Whether it was a lack of knowledge or maybe the accumulation of false knowledge about bipolar disorder (for I was never educated about it in school and only knew about it from popular culture), I intensely stigmatized it. People with bipolar disorder were 'crazy', and I was not. With each passing day, and with each pill consumed, I felt further and further away from being understood. I was increasingly more alone, trapped with my thoughts and feelings but fearful of articulating them to anyone lest they be used against me to further solidify my diagnosis. I might as well have been locked up in a padded cell and shackled, for that was exactly the way I felt.[49]*

> *... [My parents] died believing that they had brought deficient children into the world. They died believing that they were fundamentally flawed, perhaps even irresponsible in becoming parents. When they were here, I tried to tell them that it wasn't their fault: that none of us could have predicted our fate. It was never enough. Psychiatry was too powerful and our insecurities intertwined with its diagnostic labels to keep us locked into our shameful dance.[50]*

But it is not impossible:

> *I no longer identify with my previous role as a severely mentally ill psychiatric patient but a human being that is experiencing and surviving life in my own unique way ... just like every other human being on this planet.*[51]

I hope that this book will help to give people the confidence to make the choice to release themselves from the power of these labels, if they wish to do so.

So far, we have argued that any alternative to psychiatric diagnosis needs to be based on an understanding of personal meaning within its relationship and social contexts. It needs to provide an explanation that makes sense, leads to helpful ways forward, and gives hope for recovery. It needs to convey the message that people in distress have many strengths and can take responsibility for their lives, *and* they are not to blame for their difficulties.

This is a tall order, and there is no easy solution – but the next chapter will suggest some ways forward.

Chapter 7

An alternative to psychiatric diagnosis – Finding your own story

> What happens if we listen at a far deeper level to what
> people actually say about their experiences (even of severe
> distress) instead of seeing their mental lives primarily as
> a vehicle for advancing our own categories and theories?
> What if we took people's own accounts not as gibberish,
> or as some kind of code for us to decipher, but instead
> as meaningful and accurate (even if fragmentary and
> contradictory) ways of making sense of their own minds
> and life histories?[1] (Gail Hornstein)

The recovery model – pros and cons

A currently popular concept in mental health services is that
of 'recovery'. It has been defined as 'a deeply personal, unique
process of changing one's attitudes, values, feelings, goals,
skills and/or roles … A way of living a satisfying, hopeful
and contributing life even within the limitations caused by
illness'.[2] This model is official policy in mental health services
in the UK[3] and in other countries as well.

The recovery model has led to some interesting
research into common themes in the personal stories of
service users who consider themselves to have recovered.
One analysis of published accounts written by people who
had been diagnosed with 'schizophrenia' summarised the
themes as: finding hope, re-establishment of identity, finding
meaning in life, and taking responsibility for recovery.[4]
Similar results emerged from a review of the literature
on recovery from 'mental illness' in general. These were:

connectedness (including support from others and feeling part of the community); hope and optimism about the future (including belief that recovery is possible); identity (including overcoming stigma); finding meaning in life (including from the experience of 'mental illness'); and empowerment (including taking personal responsibility, focusing on strengths, and taking control of one's life).[5]

Readers will have spotted that the recovery themes are more or less the exact opposite of the messages conveyed by receiving a psychiatric diagnosis in the first place. This is a very curious aspect of the recovery vision. While it is officially described as a process of re-learning to live a meaningful life alongside the limitations of your *illness*, it does not acknowledge that what people seem to be describing is, to a large extent, recovery from the effects of the *diagnosis*. The core recovery themes are, one might say, the opposite or antidote to the devaluing, excluding, despairing, disempowering and stigmatising messages that the mental health service itself has imposed.

The recovery model was originally conceived of as an alternative to the medical one. However, when used by policy makers and professionals it is frequently seen as running alongside the traditional approach. This seems to place service users in a paradoxical position. Firstly, they are expected to accept and agree with their diagnosis, and then, a few years or decades later, to find their own way of undoing its damaging messages. This is despite research showing that accepting these labels generally means that you will do worse in the long term: 'People who accept that they have mental illness may feel driven to conform to an image of incapacity and worthlessness, becoming more socially withdrawn and adopting a disabled role. As a result, their symptoms may persist and they may become dependent on treatment providers and others ... [leading to] poor outcome.'[6]

The mental health service user/survivor movement

Recovery models originally emerged out of the wider mental health service user/survivor movement, which took off in the UK in the 1980s (see summary by Peter Beresford in *A Straight Talking Introduction to Being a Mental Health Service User*).[7] It is a curious fact that psychiatry is the only branch of medicine that has generated a significant worldwide protest movement of patients who are deeply dissatisfied with the current system and want fundamental reform. As one writer says, 'there have never been any anti-oncologists, anti-cardiologists, anti-gastroenterologists or even anti-obstetricians.'[8] Their demands include, but are certainly not limited to, changing the language we use to describe people's difficulties. Many see themselves as having been damaged rather than helped by psychiatry, and indicate this by describing themselves as 'survivors' rather than 'patients' or 'clients'.

A central principle of service user/survivor activity is that people who have been on the receiving end of psychiatric care need to have their voices heard. Professionals may be 'experts by profession' but service users should have equal status as 'experts by experience'. Some progress has been made in the UK; services are obliged to consult them, and they provide representatives to government working parties, committees drawing up research guidelines, and so on. There is an ongoing debate about the extent to which this is mere tokenism.

Historically, it has always been a struggle for service users to have their voices heard, and it is no different today. Their perspective is often dismissed as 'anecdotal' – a disrespectful term which I believe should be replaced with 'personal testimony'. This dismissal is ironic, given that the stories that they often tell, of the devastating effects of abuse, trauma, neglect, victimisation, poverty, discrimination, loss and so on, are much more solidly based on what we know about the causes of mental distress than any of the official theories.

Reclaiming your identity from psychiatry has always been a core aspect of the service user/survivor movement, as described by Peter Beresford (Chapter 6).[9] Deciding to give up your diagnosis, or perhaps to hold it cautiously and tentatively alongside other explanations, will set you free to embark on the difficult journey of finding, or reclaiming, your own story.

Telling a different story

As we saw in Chapter 4, there is a huge and growing amount of research demonstrating that difficulties and adversities of all kinds, especially in childhood, greatly increase the likelihood that people will break down. In other words, people become mentally distressed – even in the more serious cases that are labelled 'psychosis' – for good reasons. Many people learn to survive by cutting off from overwhelming feelings in various ways, particularly by a mechanism called dissociation. In this, memories become fragmented and may emerge in the form of low mood, voices, unusual beliefs, constant anxiety and sense of threat, and so on.[10,11] So-called 'symptoms' may be better understood as creative survival strategies that helped people to cope, but have outlived their usefulness.

The underlying reasons for distress aren't always immediately apparent, to either the person or the professionals, but it doesn't mean they are not there. It means that instead of asking 'What is wrong with you?' we need to ask 'What has happened to you?' Finding your own story is the process of working out what those reasons are, and how they have combined to result in your particular form of distress. It also means exploring and understanding the personal meaning that those events had to you.

At this point, people sometimes object that 'Not everyone who is abused/bullied/living in poverty develops a mental health problem'. That is true. It is not so much the circumstances themselves that are crucial – although some events will be distressing to almost everyone – but their personal meaning to the individual. To take an example, a child who was sexually abused by a neighbour, but was able to confide in warm, supportive parents and be believed and looked after and told that it was not their fault, is much less likely to suffer long-term damage than someone who was abused in secret by a parent or carer who isolated, punished and blamed them. The first child will learn that even if bad things happen, they will be loved, protected and valued. The latter child may learn to fear close relationships and to feel guilty, ashamed and worthless. Sadly, this second child will then be less able to protect and care for themselves as an adult, and will be vulnerable to further trauma and abuse.

Some people have not experienced specific traumas, but come from backgrounds where there was constant criticism or hostility or neglect which gradually undermined their sense of self-worth. Others may fail to recognise that what happened to them was in fact damaging, because it seemed normal to them at the time – for example, physical abuse that was described as 'discipline', or being sent away to school at a very young age, or perhaps feeling they have to live up to impossibly high standards.

And it is important to remember that all of us live in a culture which is, in many ways, emotionally unhealthy. Many of us are isolated from family support, unable to find a job or decent housing, struggling to make ends meet, in a society that seems to value achievement above kindness, money above welfare, and individualism above community. Recent research has shown that the bigger the income gap between the richest and poorest in a society, the higher the rates of all kinds of social ills including rates of 'mental illness'. 'If Britain became as equal as the four most equal societies … mental illness might be more than halved.'[12] This reminds us not to cast blame for anyone's breakdown – we are all, to a greater or lesser degree, doing our best within very challenging circumstances. The evidence shows that secure and loving relationships in our early lives are the best way of helping us to cope with later difficulties. However, families can only provide this kind of environment if they themselves are supported, and all of us, even the most fortunate and resilient, are vulnerable to running into trouble at some point if we live in an unfair and unequal society. Ultimately, social justice is our most powerful weapon against mental distress.

Having said this, we cannot ignore individual distress while we wait for social change. In the meantime, there is a great deal of evidence that the process of creating one's own story, or narrative, can be a helpful and healing process. For example, adults who are able to put together a coherent account about a difficult childhood are more able to come to terms with its effects, and avoid passing them on to their own children.[13] The impact of war and torture is lessened if people are supported to place their experiences within a personal account of what happened to them.[14] The development of a meaningful story about a person's voices is an essential first step in reclaiming one's life and identity.[15] The 'communicative act of bearing witness to traumatic events not only transforms traumatic memories into narratives that can … be integrated into the survivor's sense of self and view of the world … [but] also reintegrates the survivor into a community, re-establishing bonds of trust and faith in others.'[16]

I will now describe various ways of creating a narrative, or personal story.

Psychological formulation

One version of a narrative is already part of the core training and work of clinical psychologists, and is therefore available to anyone who is referred to one of them. It is known as 'psychological formulation'.[17]

Formulation is the process by which two people, a psychologist and a service user, together create a theory or 'best guess' about the origins of the difficulties that have brought the person into services. The formulation is made up of the psychologist's clinical and research knowledge – for example, evidence about the possible effects of trauma or neglect or abuse – and the service user's expertise in their own life. It might take the form of a couple of paragraphs, or sometimes a diagram, which describe how the person's relationships, social circumstances and life events have come together to lead to the current problems. The core of a formulation is working out the particular meaning of these events and contexts to you as an individual. Unlike diagnosis, this is not about making an expert judgement, but about working closely with an individual to develop a shared understanding which will evolve over time. And, again unlike diagnosis, a formulation is not based on deficits – the things that are supposedly wrong with you – but draws attention to talents and strengths in surviving what are nearly always very challenging life situations. The development of this personal story or narrative has been described by clinical psychologists as 'a process of ongoing collaborative sense-making'.[18]

Here is an invented example of a formulation for 'Jane' which would be developed jointly over a period of time, and revised and updated as the work progresses. Jane is 32 and has a daughter aged 7. Jane's father left when she was 3, and she was sexually abused by her mother's new partner from the ages of 7 to 14. She was isolated and unhappy at school and started self-harming at age 11. She had a daughter with her husband, Steve, but left him because of his physical violence towards her, and is now a single parent. When her daughter reached the age of 7, Jane's self-harming worsened and she became very depressed. She might well be diagnosed with 'borderline personality disorder'.

Possible formulation: *Your father's departure when you were at a vulnerable age was very hard for your mother to cope with, and to you it felt like a major rejection. When your stepfather began to abuse you, his threats and the fear of being blamed stopped you from telling anyone. Instead, you carried hidden feelings of guilt, anger and shame inside. Cutting yourself seemed to relieve these feelings temporarily when you couldn't express them in any other way. Desperate to find love and security, you often ended up with men who treated you badly. This simply confirmed your feelings of rejection and failure. You showed great courage in leaving your husband, and you very much want to give your daughter a better start in life. However, when she reached the age that your own abuse started, you could no longer push your feelings away. You were overwhelmed with anger and distress, and self-harm was the only thing that gave you any relief. Because of the rejections and insecurity in your past, you have great difficulty in trusting professionals, especially when they seem to be trying to control you. This simply reinforces your fears about being abused by people in a position of power over you. Despite everything you have been through, you want to overcome your difficulties and use your strength and determination to build a different life for yourself.*

We can see that the formulation is personal to Jane, and helps to make sense of her experiences in terms of what has happened to her. It suggests an individual pathway forward, which will probably include developing a trusting relationship with a worker or therapist, learning ways to manage her self-harm, perhaps gaining support from others with similar experiences, and talking through her past. It does not see Jane as a helpless victim of an illness or a personality flaw, and neither does it blame her for her situation; instead it shows how she used her strengths to survive as best she could, and how she can be supported to take further steps.

In other words, a good formulation helps us to escape from the 'brain or blame', 'chemistry or character' trap. It helps us to find a middle ground which acknowledges what someone had to do to survive, and at the same time, shows them how they can start to take control of their life again. The overall message of every formulation is: 'If anyone else had had the same experiences, they might well have reacted in the same way that you did. You are experiencing a normal reaction to an abnormal situation. You, like others, can recover.'

Psychological formulation approaches all forms of distress with the assumption that 'at some level it all makes sense'.[19] This is, as we have seen, exactly the opposite of the psychiatric assumption that 'symptoms' are the result of biological dysfunction of some sort. In my view, the work of every professional, whatever their training, should be based on this principle: that however unusual, confusing, overwhelming or frightening someone's thoughts, feelings and behaviours are, *there is a way of making sense of them.* This includes the experiences that are sometimes labelled as 'psychotic', although voices, visions and unusual beliefs often express their messages symbolically, not literally, and it can take quite a lot of joint work to clarify their meaning.

The central task of all mental health professionals is *to work alongside service users to create meaning out of chaos and despair.* From this perspective, so-called 'symptoms' are better understood as survival strategies. Voices and visions, as we will see, are often a way of surviving emotionally overwhelming experiences. Extreme anxiety and 'paranoia' often begin as responses to actual dangers. High moods can be a way of escaping crippling self-doubt, and so on. All of these strategies are useful and necessary at a time of crisis; the problem arises when we rely on them long after they have outlived their purpose. It is as if our minds and bodies are still defending themselves against threat, because we have not been able to process the original events. This kind of understanding, sometimes called a 'trauma-informed' model, is gradually gaining a hold in some psychiatric services as an alternative to the medical one.

Formulation has traditionally been used within individual or family therapy, as described above. However, not all service users want, need or are in a state to make use of therapy. In this situation, a more helpful approach may be the growing practice of team formulation. In this, a whole team or group of staff works together to construct a shared formulation about the service user's difficulties, based on the same principles outlined above. It has been reported that this is a powerful way of shifting team cultures away from a narrow biomedical approach.[20]

The main purpose of a formulation is to provide a guide to the best way forward. Initial studies and reports suggest that formulation may have a number of other benefits, both for service users (e.g., strengthening the therapeutic alliance, helping the service user to feel understood and contained, normalising problems, and increasing a sense of hope) and for professionals (e.g., reducing blame and disagreement, encouraging a collaborative approach, dealing with core issues, and increasing empathy).[21] More research needs to be done to explore and confirm these findings and expand our knowledge of how to use formulation most effectively.

Like any other approach, the usefulness of formulation depends on how you do it. Clinical psychologists' professional guidelines state that formulation practice should be collaborative; respectful of service users' views about accuracy and helpfulness; expressed in ordinary and accessible language; culturally sensitive; aware of the possible role of trauma; non-blaming; and inclusive of strengths and achievements.[22] Psychologists are expected to take a thoughtful and reflective stance which reduces the risk of using formulation in insensitive, non-consenting or disempowering ways. There is also a strong emphasis on the wider context of formulation. This includes recognising 'the possible role of services in compounding the difficulties'[23] and having 'a critical awareness of the wider societal context within which formulation takes place'.[24]

The most important and controversial issue is whether formulation is used as an addition to, or an alternative to, psychiatric diagnosis. Psychiatrists are also required in their training to 'demonstrate the ability to construct formulations of patients' problems that include appropriate differential diagnoses'.[25] While this does suggest a greater willingness to acknowledge psychosocial aspects of people's problems, the overall result is simply to add a layer to the basic biomedical model. A psychiatrist who followed these training guidelines might thus produce a formulation which looked something like this: 'schizophrenia/psychosis triggered by the stress of job loss'.

It was for this reason that the *Good Practice Guidelines on the use of Psychological Formulation* for clinical psychologists draw a clear distinction between psychiatric formulation and psychological formulation – the former being an *addition* to diagnosis, and the latter being an *alternative*. In other words, psychological formulation as practised by UK clinical psychologists 'is not premised on a functional psychiatric diagnosis (e.g., schizophrenia, personality disorder)'.[26] The argument is that if a formulation can provide a reasonably complete explanation for the experiences that have led to a psychiatric diagnosis – low mood, hearing voices, unusual beliefs and so on – then there is no place or need for an extra theory that says '… and by the way, she has schizophrenia as well'. The diagnosis becomes redundant. In the words of clinical psychologist Richard Bentall: 'Once these complaints have been explained, there is no ghostly disease remaining that also requires an explanation.'[27]

Best-practice psychological formulation is, therefore, based on fundamentally different principles from psychiatric diagnosis. It is the difference between the basic messages: 'You have a medical illness with mainly biological causes' and 'Your problems are an understandable emotional response to your life circumstances'.

Constructs

A parallel version of formulation has been developed outside mental health services by the Hearing Voices Network, a thriving self-help organisation that has branches all over the UK and in over 30 countries worldwide. Its founding members, psychiatrist Marius Romme and science journalist Sandra Escher, found that 'Patients diagnosed with schizophrenia were able to relate their experience of hearing voices to stressful and traumatic events in their life history. Patients could then begin to cope with them and start living their lives again.'[28] 'Constructs' help to show how unusual experiences actually make sense in the context of someone's life history, even if it takes a while to discover their meaning.

This is an example of a construct:

A 16-year-old girl was hearing a male voice, calling itself Erichem, which said deeply unpleasant things to her. In the background she would hear other voices that wanted to help her, but which were simply not powerful enough … She had been hearing the male voice since she was 14 years old, and it made her very angry. It first appeared when she was having problems with her father. He wanted her to do better at school and kept her on a tight rein. Erichem seemed to have the same approach to her.

Construct: The voices started when she was in puberty and having a lot of problems with her father. She was not allowed to be herself at a time when she was searching for her own identity. She felt powerless. Her father made her angry because he wanted to run her life for her, but she was not allowed to express that anger towards him. Erichem did the same thing – made her angry – and in this way the voice became a metaphor for her father. When the voice was present, she opposed him by swearing back at him, but this made the voice more negative. This is exactly what happened with her father. She could not discuss with either her father or the voices what they were saying to her, but could only become afraid or hostile. There were strong similarities between the voices' comments and criticisms and what her father used to say.[29]

The construct points towards the need to resolve the girl's feelings about her father and find a way of asserting herself. It also, like psychological formulation, looks for meanings that may be metaphorical not literal, and expressed via experiences that are sometimes called 'psychotic'.

Constructs differ from formulations in that within the Hearing Voices approach, the service user's preferred explanation is accepted even if it lies outside conventional psychological understandings. Thus, a belief in witchcraft, aliens, telepathy, gods or ghosts is treated with as much respect as any other, and valued if it is useful to the voice-hearer. Another difference, in keeping with the self-help ethos of the organisation, is that constructs do not have to be created with professional help; the support of a friend, another voice-hearer, or a self-help group serves just as well.[30] A similar approach has been applied to unusual beliefs.[31]

Writing your own story: Rachel and Fay

There are many ways of writing your own story, and a growing number of former service users are doing this for themselves. The process is beautifully described by former service user Rachel Waddingham:

> Whenever we talk about ourselves we tell stories. Without these stories, our experiences would sit – unconnected – like a thousand tiny beads. Telling our story helps us to weave connections between these beads, linking them together with different threads to create a tapestry full of meaning. This is a fluid and continually evolving process. Each new experience, interaction or connection reveals new aspects of the picture we are continually creating. It shifts and changes as we, ourselves, shift and change.
>
> Reflecting our experience of the world, this process can be terrifying and confusing as well as beautiful and rewarding. In psychiatry, something profound happens to these stories. It's as if someone takes your tapestry, labels it as defective and gives you the pattern you need to rectify your mistakes. Unquestioningly, you unpick your tapestry and – instead – weave the beads together to form a picture of symptoms, diagnosis, illness, genetic vulnerabilities and pathological responses to stress. With each stitch, those around you nod and praise your keen insight. After a while you forget that you ever had a story of your own. In this way, a 'schizophrenic' is born ...

It was at university that my inner world first began to seep out through the cracks and show itself to others ... It was at this point that I was given an alternative – a new pattern to help impose some order on the chaos. It was at this point that I became a 'schizophrenic'. In the hospital I met many kind mental health professionals who gently reassured me that I was psychotic – that my complex and frightening beliefs about my experiences were 'primary delusions' and that the alien and the bugs were simply 'hallucinations', products of my unbalanced brain chemistry and my intolerance to stress. On adopting this new perspective I felt relief – the medical lexicon stripped my experiences of their power and removed any need to further explore their meaning. Content that my tapestry was complete I put down my needle and focused on living with the illness I now knew I had ... Of all the beliefs that I have had about my experiences, the belief that I was 'schizophrenic' was the most damaging ...

Years later, officially disabled and dubbed a 'revolving door', it was clear that I was stuck. After more than 20 admissions to the unit, the illness I believed I had periodically beat down the medication I was taking to keep it under control. Without meeting the Hearing Voices Network I believe I would still be sitting there – accepting my fate as a severely and enduringly mentally ill young woman. The peer support group I attended gave me something truly precious – a safe space to begin to find my own way of describing, and making sense of, my experiences. After years of parroting the biomedical picture I'd been given ('Hi, my name is Rachel and I'm a schizophrenic'), I met people who wanted to know more. Slowly and tentatively, I began to unpick the medical tapestry and began to weave my own story once more.[32]

The *DSM-5* debate has opened up new horizons for those whose lives have been affected by psychiatric diagnosis. Fay Thomas vividly describes the despair of being overshadowed by psychiatry and the exhilaration of sensing the possibility of freedom and rewriting her and her family's story:

> I am excited. Almost as excited as I was the day the Berlin wall fell or Nelson Mandela was released from jail. For me, the current debate around the utility of the DSM-5 and psychiatric diagnosis feels that big. It feels that big because I have been personally touched by a madness from which I was told I would never recover. My only sibling has likewise lived in the shadows of diagnosis, similarly labelled and without any real hope for much of his life. I was labelled 'bipolar 1' and he as 'schizophrenic'.
>
> I'm excited by ... the breathtaking possibilities within the charge that psychiatric diagnoses lack validity. If mental illness is not primarily caused by biology I'm left wondering if I'm a fairly normal person after all? What if I'm someone who was extremely distressed at times or someone who just has bigger moods than most? That seems a bit like saying that some people tan more easily in the sun than others. And so what if they do?
>
> It might mean that my family was like many other families, except that we were stressed. Most of us were distressed and two of us got labels. Certainly the criss-cross double-bind communication within my family could have driven anybody mad. Perhaps, more tellingly, we couldn't talk about our distress and it had to be hidden. Well-functioning middle-class people weren't expected to behave that way. While our genes may have made 'madness' more likely is that really so bad? ...
>
> If psychologists are right that the primary causes of mental illness are psychosocial rather than biological, my

family narrative can be re-written. We can emerge from
our closets of shame and take our rightful place on the
continuum of acceptable human experience ... I have
remained medication-free for the past thirteen years. I no
longer identify with the label 'Bipolar'.[33]

Reclaiming your experience

Many people's recovery is about 'a decolonising process, a reclaiming of experience' in order to 'take back authorship of their own stories' rather than the diagnostic language which has 'colonised experiences of distress and alienation'. These new stories can transform narratives based on disorders and broken brains into ones of strength and survival, as part of 'our right to define ourselves; the right to find our own voice to describe our experience and our lives'.[34]

The argument of this book is that everyone has the right to make the choices that Rachel, Fay and many others have done. Psychiatry imposes a particular way of understanding your experiences. For some people this model is a helpful one, at least in the short term, even if the claim that it is in any scientific sense an accurate or 'true' one is increasingly hard to maintain. For others it is more damaging than the problems which brought them into services in the first place. It can be very hard to distance yourself from this powerful expert verdict which has such a profound effect on people's lives. In the words of psychologist Dorothy Rowe: 'In the final analysis, power is the right to have your definition of reality prevail over all other people's definition of reality.'[35] Reclaiming your own reality, asserting the right to define your own experiences, is not easy, but it can be done.

The next chapter contains further illustrations of these themes.

Chapter 8
Personal stories

The chance to have your experiences listened to can be extraordinarily powerful. In fact, there is a theme running through recovery accounts about encountering a single person who was able to listen to your human story, validate your feelings, and then offer an alternative perspective. For many people, this was a crucial turning point.

Here are three people describing their own turning point – both within and outside psychiatric services. Stewart Hendry writes:

> *During this time there was a social worker I'll always remember, who saw what it was like for me, and ... gave me an alternative idea of what my future would be like. She was much more informal and friend-like, and treated me more like a person. We talked about the future, about doing things and relationships, and she really started me on the road to doing something about what I wanted. I think that she was one of the reasons I am at this point now, one of the turning points in my life.[1]*

Ron Coleman spent ten years in the psychiatric system diagnosed with schizophrenia, and is now a mental health trainer and campaigner.

> *The big difference was that I was introduced to a worker called Lyndsey, who visited me in hospital. Although I have*

*never thanked her for it, she probably saved my life. One
day she said: 'Ron, there is a new group in Manchester
called the Hearing Voices Group. Do you want to go?' I did.
Not because I thought it might help me, but it would get me
out of the ward. It was there that I met Anne Walton who
said to me, 'Your voices are real, accept them.' For so long
I have been told that my voices were not real ... I thought
this was revolutionary.[2]*

Eleanor Longden describes how she came into contact with
psychiatry when she started hearing voices at university:

*The psychiatrist equated voice-hearing with insanity.
I got a diagnosis of schizophrenia. With this I got the
message that I was a passive victim of pathology. I wasn't
encouraged to do anything to actively help myself. Therapy
meant drug therapy. It was hugely disempowering and
undermining, exacerbating all my doubts about myself.
And the impact was devastating because it just served to
make the voices stronger and more aggressive because
I became so frightened of them ... This all happened in a
shockingly short space of time. I went into that hospital a
troubled, confused, unhappy 18-year-old and I came out a
schizophrenic. And I was a good one. I came to embody
how psychosis should look and feel ...*

*A turning point for me came a year later when I was
referred to a new psychiatrist, Pat Bracken. The very first
time I met him he said to me, 'Hi Eleanor, nice to meet you.
Can you tell me a bit about yourself?' So I just looked at
him and said, 'I'm Eleanor and I'm a schizophrenic.' And
in his quiet, Irish voice he said something very powerful,
'I don't want to know what other people have told you
about yourself, I want to know about you.' It was the first
time that I had been given the chance to see myself as a*

person with a life story, not as a genetically determined schizophrenic with aberrant brain chemicals and biological flaws and deficiencies that were beyond my power to heal ... Pat Bracken was so much more humane than that. And he didn't talk about auditory hallucinations; he talked about hearing voices and unusual beliefs rather than delusions, anxiety rather than paranoia. He didn't use this terrible mechanistic, clinical language; he just couched it in normal language and normal experience.[3]

Eleanor then describes how she was gradually able to make sense of her distress, which included hearing a voice she believed to be demonic:

He's not coming from outside, he can't be, it can only be from me. I was very intrigued by this idea and I began to slowly realise that yes, he is a demon, but he was a personal demon. Everyone has their private demons and his demonic aspects were the unaccepted aspects of my self-image, my shadow, so it was appropriate that he was so shadowy. He'd always been dismissed as this psychotic hallucination, but even his physical form did have meaning to it. The only way I recovered was by learning this grotesque aspect of him is superfluous. The contempt and loathing that he expresses is actually to do with me in that it reflects how I feel about myself. He is like a very external form of my own insecurities, my own self-doubt, and that is the part that is relevant and does need attending to, does need taking seriously because he is meaningful. What he says is a very powerful statement about what I am feeling about myself and in that respect I do relate him to me by learning to deconstruct this figure and learn what is relevant and what isn't.

He has a lot of relevance and a lot of personal meaning and he is capable of making very powerful statements about issues in my life that I need to deal with. This included childhood abuse, as well as adulthood experiences of injustice and adversity. It is difficult because voices are often metaphorical and you need to find the literal meaning in a figurative form of speech and seek the personal relevance in it. For instance, when he talks very violently about mutilation and death I see it as a barometer and realise that I need to take better care of myself and attend to my own needs more. It sounds like a bizarre thing to say, but he is useful in that he does provide insight into conflicts that I need to deal with.

Having become more trusting of him, in turn, he became more compassionate towards me. Rather than being abusive back to him, I became more gentle and even loving towards him, and that vicious circle that we'd gotten into, of antagonism, hostility and malevolence, began to diminish. I realised that he could be a positive force if I would let him be. It took a long time, but it got to the point where my demons could be cast out. While he is still around – he has never left and he is still there – he has lost his power to devastate me. I listen to him now because I understand that I'm actually listening to me. I don't catastrophise him. I see that like when my mum gets very stressed, she gets bad headaches; when I get very stressed, I hear really bad voices. I now show respect to him and he is now more likely to show me respect. Essentially, this represents taking a more compassionate, empathic and forgiving stance towards myself. ...

It is now many years since I last took medication or needed support from mental health services. I live a high-functioning, high-achieving life. I have a partner, my own home, many close friends, and I recently obtained the highest degree in psychology my university had ever awarded. I am weary of romanticising psychosis, and *although what happened was terrible, I am glad that it happened because emotionally I was stuck and it gave me the chance to move on. It wasn't a breakdown, it was a breakthrough.*

Rufus May describes his journey into and out of 'paranoia', or suspicious thoughts, and the sense he now makes of it. He now practises as a clinical psychologist.

At the age of 18 I found myself in a boring job as an office junior. I was anxious about my future – I had failed in education and I had failed to get into the advertising business. On top of this, emotionally I was struggling to adjust to the fact that my first girlfriend, who I had been with for a year, had left me. This left a big hole in my life. In hindsight this emotional loss echoed an earlier experience of abandonment I'd had when I was 11 years old: my mother had had a brain haemorrhage and had suffered some brain damage. Although she had recovered, she had some personality changes which I found difficult to adapt to ... Also, I found myself socially isolated: my best friend was in Germany and I was trying to avoid my former dope-smoking friends ...

Instead of getting depressed I gradually entered an alternative reality that had spiritual undertones. My experiences also included the television and radio talking to me and beliefs that I was a spy, involved in a science-fiction-like battle between Russia and England. I was eventually admitted to hospital after I complained that I had a gadget in my chest that was being used to control me.

I found hospital treatment very oppressive ... Nobody talked to me about my experiences and ideas. They thought this would encourage them and make them worse. Because my grandfather and aunt had been given diagnoses of schizophrenia, doctors were convinced I had a condition they assumed was genetic ... My rebellious nature was helpful in that I refused to accept the schizophrenia diagnosis ... I had a strong story of hope in my family. I had witnessed my mother making a strong recovery from her brain haemorrhage and resulting disability through a combination of her own will and determination and support from others. I think I used this as a blueprint for my own recovery. I sought out community centres, churches, drama classes and later dance classes as places to connect with others and express myself ... At the same time I was always convinced that my ideas and experiences made sense in some way. I gradually came to see them as an emotional reaction to the break-up of my relationship with my first girlfriend, which had triggered some deeper emotional conflicts.

Since my breakdown in my late teens, I have been pretty healthy, physically and emotionally. It was as if it released something for me and allowed me to make important changes to how I live my life.[4]

Laura Delano describes her 13-year psychiatric history and how she eventually escaped it:

As a fourteen-year-old, I hated the world, and I hated myself. This hatred stemmed from a realization I'd had while looking in the mirror at the start of my eighth grade year: that everything I thought I knew about who I was, where I belonged, and what I believed in, was not as it seemed. In the snap of a finger, anything tenable was untenable; any person I'd once trusted was untrustworthy; any characteristic of mine that had made me the girl I'd become in my first thirteen years on the planet was suddenly inauthentic and fake ... I was a fraud, and a puppet being directed by greater social forces.

My social circles had changed, and I'd begun to spend time with a more marginalized and less straight-and-narrow group of girls. I was confused, disoriented even, and I felt trapped. Trapped by my town and my school, by the social standards I'd been raised to never question, by the reputation I felt I'd had to uphold for as long as I could remember. I was a prisoner in my own skin, years and years of an identity built up around an empty core.

In revolt, I began to question everything that had been taught to me by my parents, my school, and my town. It was quite destabilising and disorienting to believe that everything I once held as real actually wasn't, and quickly, my confusion and fear morphed into anger channeled at any person who had tried to 'make' me who I was. It didn't help that this anger was brought to a psychiatrist, who told me at the end of our first session that the rage was a symptom of 'mania', and that I was 'bipolar'. Fuck that, I thought, the fire inside of me burning brightly. No way am I crazy.

Flash forward four years, when, as a freshman in college, I found myself utterly desperate for someone to tell me who I was, what was wrong with me, and what I needed to do to fix it. Indeed, I had turned one-hundred-and-eighty degrees. Prescriptions for Depakote and Prozac had chased me through high school, as had that 'bipolar' label, which I'd shunned, agreeing to a 'major depression' label instead ... I was ready to 'turn myself in' to psychiatry, convinced that I couldn't manage my emotions, my thoughts, or myself, any longer. It didn't matter that I'd been a successful student and athlete, a writer, a lover of nature, and a reliable friend, or that I was privileged with four years ahead of me at a prestigious college; I was in so much emotional and existential pain that I was sure I was broken, that the psychiatrist had been right all along ...

I surrendered myself immediately to a psychiatrist at America's most prestigious private psychiatric institution, and became a full-blooded patient, passive and dependent and convinced of her brokenness, in a matter of weeks. I believed him when he said I'd need 'meds' for the rest of my life, and would have to learn how to 'manage my symptoms' and 'set realistic expectations' for myself. I was sure that the 'bipolar' diagnosis was the explanation for all my problems, and that the prescribed 'treatment' would be my solution. I needed to be 'bipolar', and I needed to want the antipsychotic, antidepressant, and sleeping pill prescriptions that were written for me at the end of that first session, because they gave me hope that something could, and would, change …

It meant surrendering my humanness and replacing it with the narrative of a 'chemical imbalance, of an abnormal 'condition' that made me different from everyone around me. It meant sacrificing my agency, my sense of self, and my sense of responsibility and accountability to the DSM, to any proclamation made by a 'mental health professional', and to my 'meds'. It meant that I stopped trusting my gut, following my instincts, or having faith in myself and my ability to feel big feelings or think intense thoughts, and that my psychiatrist was always on speed dial in case I needed an upped dosage or an extra therapy session when I sensed another 'episode' coming on. It meant that I was fragile, 'couldn't handle' too much stress, was emotionally unpredictable … was hypersensitive, and was at the whim of my disease; indeed being bipolar became my justifiable excuse for impulsive behaviors, fights with family or friends, and shirked responsibilities.

It meant that I was bipolar.

… And how, just how, did I wake up? Let me focus, for the time being, on The Moment. *That is, the moment in*

which I began to wake up from thirteen years of drugged, numbed, disconnected, psychiatrically labeled sleep ... You see, in that critical moment in May 2010, the spark that years ago had been fiery and bright in me was once again rekindled, the fuel, Robert Whitaker's Anatomy of an Epidemic. Upon seeing its hardcover face looking at me from a 'New Release' shelf in a Vermont bookstore, I couldn't have predicted in my wildest imaginings that the result would be an awakening; indeed, I was so anesthetized by psychiatry's spell that I didn't even know I was asleep. But something in the deepest parts of me – my life force, my élan vital – was stirring, and desperate for change. I was in an existential survival mode, although I didn't know it consciously, and I was ready for something to be the catalyst. The timing was just right for it to be Anatomy, and despite how incredibly disconnected and sedated my mind was from five psychotropic drugs, my human spirit, still in me after all those years under the 'care' of psychiatry, began to stir.

I know today that my spirit was in me all along, small and faded and hidden away, but patiently waiting for the chance to wake up ... Something inside of me was desperate for change, for a path that would lead me away from where I was in that moment ... and all it took was an openness, and a readiness, to try out a different way of thinking. It was a way of thinking that required I leave behind every single belief I held about myself – that I was 'mentally ill', that I had a 'chemical imbalance', and that I needed 'medication' to 'treat' this 'condition' that made me eternally different ... At the root of it all, I needed to be ready and open to the idea that, in truth, there had never been anything wrong inside of me, that I was no different than any other person, and that the intense emotional and psychic pain I'd felt for much of my life was not a *'symptom' to be 'treated', but rather, was a part of the vast spectrum of human experience, as well as the direct result of entering the 'mental health' system in the first place ...*

If you're out there and you believe in your deepest depths that your suffering is a manifestation of a life-long illness that requires a life-long relationship to psychiatric drugs, there is an alternative story. There are many alternative stories. For a long time, I believed psychiatry when it told me who I was and what my future held for me, and this 'mental illness' narrative kept me dehumanized and mired in a place of darkness, hopelessness, and disconnection ... When I started to ask questions ... I discovered that my humanity and a future of connection to self and world were waiting for me, if I was willing to let go of my illness narrative and walk through the fear of the unknown – of who I was beyond a psychiatric diagnosis and a bottle of pills, which had long been all I was. It's been a confusing, painful, beautiful, and continuously unfolding journey back to myself since that time, and ... I am so profoundly grateful.[5]

Commentary

These stories are a powerful demonstration of what has been called 'the restorative power of truth-telling'.[6] They show that 'Just as the self can be undone and dehumanised by brutality and isolation it can be renewed and remade through solidarity and connection with others through narrative.'[7]

You may, like Eleanor and Stewart, find this kind of opportunity within services. Outside the mental health system, this kind of work has been one of the most powerful aspects of the service user/survivor movement.

Getting together in groups provides a chance for service users to have safe discussions with others who have been through similar situations, without any sense of being judged, without having to worry what others will think of them, without the assumption that they must be 'mad' or 'weird' or 'strange'. It can make it possible for them for the first time to talk freely and openly about what they have been through.[8]

Two former service users, Jacqui Dillon and Rufus May, who have been through this process themselves and now support others to tread the same path, have described the process by which people can be supported in 'reclaiming their experience in order to take back authorship of their own stories'.[9] They acknowledge that for some people, the medical narrative is a helpful one. Others may prefer socio-political, spiritual or paranormal explanations, and that is their right. In contrast to psychiatry, 'Our guiding principle has been that each person knows how best to proceed in understanding their experience … everyone has inherent expertise and wisdom about their life.' Their groupwork is about 'finding a space where one can tell one's story, discover one's truths and explore possible ways forward'.[10]

Not everyone can easily access the support to do this kind of work, but the final chapter will suggest some possibilities.

Chapter 9
Next steps in developing a personal story

Some people find that just realising that there are good reasons for their breakdown is enough to start the process of rebuilding their lives. However, most will need support to do this, either within or outside mental health services. In the current psychiatric system there are no easy ways to find this, but here are some thoughts.

As a service user: Be careful

Anyone who has decided that they do not want or agree with their psychiatric diagnosis will need to be quite cautious about whether and how they act on this. It is all too easy to be told that you are 'lacking in insight' which may lead to consequences like delayed discharge from hospital, forced medication and so on. You may need to go along with a diagnosis for practical reasons like accessing benefits and in order to maintain a good relationship with your mental health team – or at least, not get into open conflict with them. However, and this is the central message of this book: *You do not need to take on the diagnosis as part of your identity.* You no longer need to see yourself as 'mentally ill', 'personality disordered', 'bipolar', 'psychotic' or whatever. Most of the people whose stories appear in this book have never been officially 'undiagnosed'. They simply made the important personal decision that they were not going to see themselves or their problems in this way.

But, as Ron Coleman admits, this is not an easy process.

> In the early 1980s I was diagnosed as schizophrenic ... In
> 1993 I gave up being schizophrenic and decided to be Ron
> Coleman. Undoing the messages of diagnosis means taking
> back responsibility for yourself; it means that you can no
> longer blame your illness for your actions. It means there
> is no disease to hide behind ... but more important than all
> these things it means that you stop being a victim of your
> experience and start being the owner of your experience.[1]

Laura Delano faced the same challenges:

> When I found liberation in my own mental health recovery
> and gained the confidence required to shed the costume
> I'd been wearing as a 'good patient' for all those years, I
> realized that I'd have to face the fear of the unknown – of
> owning my feelings, taking responsibility for my actions,
> of facing emotional discomfort without retreating, and of
> discovering who I really was underneath it all. It required
> faith, less so in myself in the beginning and more so in
> other people, because I needed to trust that if others in the
> recovery community had once been as lost and hopeless
> and empty as I was but no longer were, the same was
> possible for me, too.[2]

As a friend or family member: Be supportive

Families and friends may, with the best of intentions, have
accepted their relative's diagnosis as the 'truth' and they too
may find it hard to adjust to a new perspective.

> While carers of the mentally ill are naturally concerned
> for their well-being, they may disenfranchise the patient.

> *In my own case, my family, although I love them, find it hard to accept even now that I am now healed and as well as they are – they persist in seeing me as vulnerable, as schizophrenic. We can become trapped in others' perceptions of us and find it hard to move on.*[3]

For a relative, revising your views on diagnosis may be hard, but it will put you in a better position to offer support and a listening ear to a family member who also wants to rethink how they see their problems.

Friends can also be extremely valuable in this role, as Rufus May found:

> *During my second admission my close friend Catherine returned from abroad and started to visit me … She showed me an acceptance that was deeply healing. She believed I would get through this 'breakdown' and make a recovery. Her positive and accepting approach had a dramatic effect on my attitude towards my situation.*[4]

Rufus was eventually able to make sense of his experiences 'through a number of conversations with different friends'.

As a professional: Be open-minded

Some psychiatrists have argued for a 'narrative view of psychiatry' in which 'the most important task for the psychiatrist is to engage with [service users'] stories respectfully and empathically'.[5] Professionals can support service users in this work whatever their own personal views about diagnosis. It will be easier to do this if you are willing to consider and inform yourself about alternative viewpoints as described in this book.

From a wider perspective, the arguments in this book imply that professionals of all backgrounds need to face some tough questions about whether we should be imposing diagnostic language on people in the first place. Others – managers, policy-makers, journalists, politicians and so on – need to think about the extent to which they have colluded with this practice. There is no space to explore this further here, but I hope that all those involved in the field of mental health will be open-minded enough to give serious consideration to the broader critiques of psychiatry via the resources listed below.

Next steps

Here are some ideas for service users who may want to take next steps. While some of this applies mainly in the UK, many of these resources are more widely available.

Primary health care services (services based in the community)

You should be able to access counselling or therapy through your GP. The NHS in England runs a project called 'Improving Access to Psychological Therapies' (IAPT) which is meant to ensure that everyone who needs it is able to find a properly trained therapist. At present this is only for people who suffer from anxiety and depression, but in future the project will expand to include people with more severe difficulties such as 'psychosis'. The project is based on diagnostic categories, but it also involves the use of formulation.

By virtue of their day-to-day work experience, many GPs take a broad perspective on the nature of mental health problems and may be prepared to support you in finding a non-diagnostic perspective.

Secondary mental health services (services based in hospitals or psychiatric outpatient clinics)

Clinical psychologists use formulation, as described in Chapter 7. Waiting lists are often long, but people can ask to be referred. The same is true of counselling psychologists, who are employed in some services. While some psychologists do accept a diagnostic view, they will respect the service user's preferences, and they are all trained to help them to develop a shared formulation-based understanding.

A few psychiatrists also work in this way, especially in the case of less severe difficulties. Since formulation is part of their training too (although, as discussed, this is usually as an addition to a diagnosis) it may be worth asking them whether they are willing to consider this approach. Some may be willing to negotiate what diagnosis you are happiest with. For example, the diagnosis of 'adjustment disorder', which features in both *DSM* and *ICD*, is much less stigmatising than some other labels, and fits just about everyone, since it is defined as having difficulty coping with a current stress or life event. Another possibility is 'dissociative disorder' instead of 'psychosis' or 'schizophrenia'. This diagnosis is recognised as being a possible response to trauma and is found in *ICD* and *DSM*.

Psychiatric nurses and social workers probably won't use the term 'formulation', but many are very skilled in helping service users put together a picture of how their life circumstances have contributed to their difficulties. As with any professional, it may take time to find someone you feel comfortable with.

It may be helpful to contact a mental health advocate. They vary in their views, but it is their job to support service users in making their views known to their team, or requesting a referral to a psychologist or a review of their diagnosis. If your keyworker cannot advise you about how to contact

an advocate, you can find one via http://www.u-kan.co.uk:
'UKAN was founded in 1990 to be a national resource,
linking mental health user groups of all types. The common
aim is the use of advocacy in many forms to empower people
who use specialist services.'

Private therapy

If you can afford it, private therapy gives the option of
choosing someone who is willing to work in the way you
prefer. Many therapists will offer a free first session so that
you can decide if they are right for you.

Registered counsellors and therapists can be found through:
http://www.bacp.co.uk

Clinical psychologists can be found through:
http://www.bps.org.uk/psychology-public/find-psychologist/
find-psychologist

Voluntary and service user organisations

These organisations are often, although not always, less
tied to a diagnostic viewpoint. The ones listed below are
supportive of non-medical perspectives.

http://www.hearing-voices.org
The Hearing Voices Network offers information, support
and understanding to people who hear voices and those who
support them. It also aims to promote awareness, tolerance
and understanding of voice hearing, visions, tactile sensations
and other unusual experiences.

http://www.nationalparanoianetwork.org
Network for people who experience suspicious thoughts and
'paranoia'.

http://www.nsun.org.uk
The NSUN network for mental health is an independent, service-user-led charity that connects people with experience of mental health issues to give them a stronger voice in shaping policy and services. Includes information about service user groups, activities and resources across the country.

http://www.spiritualcrisisnetwork.org.uk
Offers an alternative perspective, practical advice and email support to people who are interested in exploring the idea of spiritual crisis. There are some local groups in London.

http://www.voicecollective.co.uk
The Voice Collective is hosted by Mind in Camden (London) and is a resource 'for young people who hear, see and sense things others don't'.

Self-help
Along with, or instead of, these suggestions, service users may wish to do more reflecting on their experiences themselves, perhaps with the support of a partner, friend or family member. The stories in this book will probably have triggered some thoughts and ideas.

There are a number of books, videos and websites about people's personal stories and their journeys to recovery. They are an invaluable source of hope and inspiration, and I strongly recommend them. Here are some suggestions:

Video testimony
http://www.igotbetter.org
A collection of videos by people who see themselves as having recovered.

http://openparadigmproject.com
The Open Paradigm Project has a collection of video
testimonies by people who have experienced various forms of
madness, and their paths out of the mental health system.

http://psychdiagnosis.weebly.com
An American website which campaigns for recognition of the
damage done by psychiatric diagnosis. It has videos and stories
from many service users about their experience of diagnosis.

http://talentsearch.ted.com/video/Eleanor-Longden-
Learning-from-t;TEDLondon
A short TED talk in which psychologist and voice-hearer
Eleanor Longden talks about her experiences.

http://www.youtube.com/watch?v=JHzHliy5yeQ
Trainer, writer and voice-hearer Jacqui Dillon describes her
experiences.

Websites
http://www.gailhornstein.com
This website includes an extensive list of first-person accounts
of madness.

http://www.madinamerica.com
This website is an invaluable resource for critical perspectives
on all aspects of mental health. It also includes inspiring blogs
by a number of former service users, some of whom have
been quoted in this book, including Laura Delano and Rachel
Waddingham.

http://www.mindfreedom.org/personal-stories
Mind Freedom aims to 'win human rights campaigns in
mental health, challenge abuse by the psychiatric drug
industry, support the self-determination of psychiatric

survivors and mental health consumers and promote safe, humane and effective options in mental health'. The website also has a large collection of personal stories.

http://www.nationalparanoianetwork.org
Website with ideas and resources for people with suspicious thoughts and paranoia.

http://www.paranoidthoughts.com
Website about 'unfounded or excessive fears about others' from Daniel Freeman, clinical psychologist and author of self-help books. Includes first-person accounts by people who have experienced suspicious thoughts and paranoia.

http://www.recoveringfrompsychiatry.com
Laura Delano's website tells the story of her recovery from 13 years in the psychiatric system, and has articles and resources.

http://studymore.org.uk/mpu.htm
This project is a fascinating history of the service user/survivor movement, including personal accounts.

Books

Cordle, H, Carson, J & Richards, P (eds) (2010) *Psychosis: Stories of recovery and hope.* London: Quay Books.

> Fifteen people tell their stories, and professionals describe various approaches to understanding and helping, including the traditional medical model as well as the recovery approach.

Geekie, J, Read, J, Randal, P & Lampshire, D (eds) (2011) *Experiencing Psychosis: Personal and professional perspectives.* London: Routledge.

> First-person accounts are examined alongside current research to suggest how personal experience

can contribute to the way that professionals try to understand and help.

Grant, A, Biley, F & Walker, H (eds) (2011) *Our Encounters with Madness.* Ross-on-Wye: PCCS Books.

> This is an edited collection of 36 service user and carer accounts of diagnosis, personal experience, and the system. The stories are frank, mixed and uncensored.

Knight, T (2013) *Beyond Belief: Alternative ways of working with delusions, obsessions and unusual experiences.* Peter Lehmann Publishing. Downloadable free from http://www.peter-lehmann-publishing.com/beyond-belief.htm

> This book offers a new way of helping people deal with unusual beliefs, by encouraging supporters to consider working within the person's belief system.

Romme, M, Escher, S, Dillon, J, Corstens, D & Morris, M (eds) (2009) *Living with Voices: 50 stories of recovery.* Ross-on-Wye: PCCS Books.

> Fifty people describe how they have overcome their problems with hearing voices, outside of the illness model, by overcoming feelings of threat and powerlessness and discovering that voices are not a sign of madness but a reaction to problems in their lives.

Reports

The Division of Clinical Psychology has published some accessible reports based on the belief that people have the right to choose their own understanding of their distress, which may or may not be a medical one, and their own preferred forms of help. The reports include comprehensive lists of resources. They can be downloaded for a small fee.

Division of Clinical Psychology (2010) *Understanding Bipolar Disorder: Why people experience extreme mood states and what can help.* Leicester: British Psychological Society. http://shop.bps.org.uk/understanding-bipolar-disorder-11448.html

Division of Clinical Psychology. *Understanding 'Depression'.* Leicester: British Psychological Society (due in 2015). Will be available at http://shop.bps.org.uk

Division of Clinical Psychology. *Understanding 'Psychosis'.* Leicester: British Psychological Society (due in late 2014). Will be available at http://shop.bps.org.uk

Use of medication

One of the main ways that medication can be helpful to people is by reducing overwhelming feelings. Obviously this has pros and cons, and in the long term, healing depends on being able to work through emotional distress in a safe and supportive environment. Drugs may interfere with this process.

As has been emphasised throughout the book, it is dangerous to reduce or stop medication suddenly, and no one should do so without advice from a prescriber. These resources may help you to think through your decision about medication, in addition to Joanna Moncrieff's *A Straight Talking Introduction to Psychiatric Drugs.*[6]

Breggin, PR (2012) *Psychiatric drug withdrawal: A guide for practitioners, therapists, patients and their families.* New York: Springer.

Coming Off Psychiatric Medication website (www.comingoff.com)

The Harm Reduction Guide to Coming Off Psychiatric Drugs is published by the Icarus Project and Freedom Center,

Some reflections on good practice in mental health … and general further reading

The cost of mental health services is extremely high – an estimated £10 billion in the UK every year.[7] This would perhaps be acceptable if it seemed to be helping people – but all the indications are that outcomes are getting worse.[8] One of the strangest facts about psychiatry is that recovery rates from the most serious difficulties – those that are diagnosed as 'psychosis' and 'schizophrenia' – are actually better in the developing world than in Western countries which rely on diagnosis, medication and the biomedical model. This has been confirmed by numerous surveys, carried out by highly respectable bodies such as the World Health Organization. The reasons are complex, but seem to be partly to do with higher levels of family and community support in some cultures, along with a greater acceptance of unusual experiences[9] and less, or no, use of medication. Another strange fact is that Moral Treatment, the compassionate, non-medical approach of the 19th century, seems to have resulted in higher rates of recovery than any modern approach.[10]

Within this generally bleak current picture, there are some reasons for hope. For example, Open Dialogue, a project in Finland based on shared dialogue and communication within family groups along with minimal or no use of medication, is currently achieving the best outcomes for 'psychosis' in the Western world.[11]

What is interesting from the point of view of the debate about diagnosis is that all of the most successful approaches, both past and present, are based on the common principle of *offering supportive relationships so that the individual can be helped to find their own personal way forward.* Diagnosis and the medical model play a marginal role, if any at all. The same principles are used in many non-Western cultures. Rather than giving one person a stigmatising label which carries strong implications of blame, dysfunction and despair, the meaning of the distress is explored through family and community rituals.

The principles which need to underpin better mental health services in the West have been summarised by the Hearing Voices Network, England, as:

Seeing mental distress as human and, ultimately, understandable: Rather than seeing voices, visions and extreme states as symptoms of an underlying illness, we believe it is helpful to view them as meaningful experiences – even if we don't yet know what that meaning is. We believe it's important to use human language when describing human experiences rather than medical terminology. Given the role of trauma and adversity, we need to start asking 'What has happened to you?' rather than 'What is wrong with you?'

Keeping the person in the driving seat: We want people to have the freedom to define their own experience. Support should be based on need, not diagnosis. Equally, people need to access a wide range of alternatives to understand and manage their experiences. Medication is just one way, amongst many, that people may choose. We need information about the pros/cons of each approach – true choice and collaboration, no coercion.

Supportive communities: Mental distress is not just the domain of mental health services. Communities have an important role to play in supporting those who are struggling to cope. Community-based options can run alongside, and as alternatives to, psychiatry. Equally, these approaches must go hand in hand with greater awareness of the causal impact of social factors such as poverty, gender and racial inequalities, unemployment, deprivation and abuse, on mental distress.[12]

Conclusion

I am very aware that this book contains some extremely challenging and controversial ideas. Reading it may be upsetting as well as, I hope, enlightening, and it is likely to lead to as much opposition as support. We are, I believe, on the brink of fundamental changes in psychiatry, and for all sorts of reasons this is bound to arouse strong feelings. I want to repeat that readers are completely free to reject the arguments in this book, in part or in whole. However, if it has enabled one service user to find a more hopeful and healing story, or one relative, friend or professional to support someone to find a new way forward, then it has fulfilled its purpose.

This book doesn't provide any easy answers. People who want to leave their diagnoses behind may still need to retain them for some practical purposes; may not be able to achieve official 'undiagnosing'; and may not be able to persuade others to support them. However, they may feel able to choose not to take their diagnosis on as part of their identity. I will end with some words from former service user Rachel Waddingham which encapsulate the spirit of this book:

My recovery has been a long and painful road ... It needed me to reject the idea of being 'ill' and reclaim my sense of being human. It needed a sense of safety, trust and hope. It needed the people around me to be ready to face my narrative unflinchingly, no matter how painful, and to believe fully that I would find a way of making sense of it. Finally, it involved me subjecting the ideas I had been sold as a patient to scrutiny and making an informed choice over whether or not to believe them.[13]

Further reading on psychiatry

If you want to find out more about critiques of psychiatry in general, and maybe participate in and campaign for some of the emerging non-diagnostic approaches, these are some starting points:

Books
All the other *Straight Talking Introductions*, plus:

Bentall, RP (2009) *Doctoring the Mind: Why psychiatric treatments fail.* London: Allen Lane/Penguin.
> A readable overview of the history and critiques of psychiatry and psychological approaches to madness by a well-known clinical psychologist.

Breggin, PR (1993) *Toxic Psychiatry*. London: Fontana.
> One of the earliest and most powerful critiques of psychiatry, by a psychiatrist.

Cromby, J, Harper, D & Reavey, P (eds) (2013) *Understanding Mental Health and Distress: Beyond abnormal psychology*. Basingstoke: Palgrave Macmillan.
> The first undergraduate textbook not to be based on diagnostic categories. Chapters by professionals and service users.

Fernando, S (2002) *Mental Health, Race and Culture* (2nd ed). Basingstoke, New York: Palgrave.

> Psychiatrist Suman Fernando critiques psychiatry from the perspective of non-Western cultures.

Herman, JL (1997) *Trauma and Recovery: From domestic abuse to political terror.* New York: Basic Books.

> A classic book about the effects of trauma. This approach informs many current approaches to 'psychosis'.

Hornstein, GA (2012) *Agnes's Jacket: A psychologist's search for the meanings of madness.* Ross-on-Wye: PCCS Books.

> Gail Hornstein's meetings with, and reflections on, people who challenge accepted views about madness.

Johnstone, L (2000) *Users and Abusers of Psychiatry: A critical look at psychiatric practice* (2nd ed). Hove, New York: Routledge.

> An accessible overview of the limitations of current practice, illustrated by real-life examples.

Johnstone, L & Dallos, R (2013) *Formulation in Psychology and Psychotherapy: Making sense of people's problems* (2nd ed). London, New York: Routledge.

> An introduction to the theory and practice of formulation, mainly intended for professionals but accessibly written.

Rapley, M, Moncrieff, J & Dillon, J (eds) (2011) *De-Medicalizing Misery: Psychiatry, psychology and the human condition.* Basingstoke: Palgrave.

> A collection of essays taking a critical perspective on psychiatry.

Read, J & Dillon, J (eds) (2013) *Models of Madness: Psychological, social and biological approaches to psychosis* (2nd ed). London, New York: Routledge.

> A very comprehensive overview of all aspects of theory and practice in mental health, from a critical perspective.

Romme, M & Escher, S (1993) (eds) *Accepting Voices.* London: MIND.

> A ground-breaking book about learning to live with voices.

Watters, E (2011) *Crazy Like Us: The globalization of the Western mind.* London: Constable & Robinson.

> An American journalist documents the devastating effects of exporting psychiatry and its assumptions to other cultures.

Whitaker, R (2010) *Anatomy of an Epidemic: Magic bullets, psychiatric drugs, and the astonishing rise of mental illness in America.* New York: Crown Publishing Group.

> An award-winning American science journalist exposes horrifying facts about the impact of psychiatric medications.

Websites

http://www.asylumonline.net
'An International Magazine for Democratic Psychiatry, Psychology and Community Development'; has articles written by service users and professionals.

http://www.behaviorismandmentalhealth.com
Retired psychologist Phil Hickey directs hard-hitting criticism at diagnosis and the 'spurious concepts' underpinning psychiatry.

http://www.behindthelabel.co.uk
Rachel Waddingham is a former service user, now a writer
and trainer. Her website has links, articles and resources.

http://beyondmeds.com
Website and blog of Monica Cassani: 'My own experience
as both (now – ex) patient and a mental health professional
allows for some interesting and sometimes uncomfortable
insights into the mental health system in the United States.' A
very comprehensive collection of resources and information.

http://www.cepuk.org
The Council for Evidence-Based Psychiatry 'exists to
communicate evidence of the potentially harmful effects of
psychiatric drugs to the people and institutions in the UK
that can make a difference, given that the scientific record
clearly shows that psychiatric medications, portrayed as safe
and effective by areas of the medical profession, often lead to
worse outcomes for many patients, particularly when taken
long term'.

http://www.critpsynet.freeuk.com
A very useful collection of articles from a broadly critical
perspective.

http://discursiveoftunbridgewells.blogspot.co.uk
'Views and commentary on psychology, mental health and
other stuff' from the Salomons Centre for Applied Psychology
at Canterbury Christ Church University. A frequent theme is
how we understand and respond to 'mental illness'.

http://www.dxsummit.org
This international website campaigns for and shares ideas
about alternatives to diagnosis.

http://www.intervoiceonline.org
Intervoice is the International Hearing Voices Network (the International Network for Training, Education and Research into Hearing Voices). It includes extensive international resources about ways of overcoming the difficulties faced by people who hear voices, as well as the more positive aspects of the experience and its cultural and historical significance.

http://www.jacquidillon.org
Jacqui Dillon is a writer, campaigner, international speaker and trainer, and also a voice-hearer. Her website has information and resources.

http://www.madinamerica.com
Site run by Robert Whitaker, author of *Mad in America* and *Anatomy of an Epidemic*. 'The site is designed to serve as a resource and a community for those interested in rethinking psychiatric care in the United States and abroad. It provides readers with news, stories of recovery, access to source documents, and the informed writings of bloggers that will further this enterprise.'

http://www.rufusmay.com
Rufus May is a clinical psychologist and trainer who has recovered from his own experience of psychosis. He wants to create alternative understandings to medical labelling. His website has details of books, magazines, training events and organisations that promote positive approaches to emotional health and recovery.

http://www.theicarusproject.net
The Icarus Project is a grassroots network of independent groups and individuals 'living with the experiences that are commonly labelled bipolar disorder'. It promotes a new culture and language that looks beyond a conventional medical model of mental illness.

Endnotes

Chapter 1

1. Page 10 in Boyle, M (2013) The persistence of medicalisation: Is the presentation of alternatives part of the problem? In S Coles, S Keenan & B Diamond (eds) *Madness Contested: Power and practice* (pp 3–22). Ross-on-Wye: PCCS Books.

2. https://www.youtube.com/watch?v=GUMY5NUhVTU

3. Harper, D (2013) On the persistence of psychiatric diagnosis. *Feminism and Psychology, 23*(1), 78–85.

4. Moncrieff, J (2010) Psychiatric diagnosis as political device. *Social Theory and Health, 8,* 370–82.

5. Timimi, S (2009) A *Straight Talking Introduction to Children's Mental Health Problems.* Ross-on-Wye: PCCS Books.

6. Laing, RD (1960) *The Divided Self.* London: Tavistock Press.

7. Szasz, T (1976) Schizophrenia: The sacred symbol of psychiatry. *British Journal of Psychiatry, 129,* 308–16.

8. Breggin, P (1993) *Toxic Psychiatry.* London: Fontana.

9. Bracken, P, Thomas, P, Timimi, S, Asen, E, Behr, G, Beuster, C, et al (2012) Psychiatry beyond the current paradigm. *British Journal of Psychiatry, 201,* 430–4.

10. Coppock, V & Hopton, J (2000) *Critical Perspectives on Mental Health.* London/New York: Routledge.

11. Kirk, SA & Kutchins, H (1997) *Making Us Crazy: DSM – The psychiatric bible and the creation of mental disorder*. New York/London: The Free Press.

12. Barker, P (2011) Psychiatric diagnosis. In P Barker (ed) *Mental Health Ethics: The human context* (pp 139–48). London/New York: Routledge.

13. Bentall, RP (2009) *Doctoring the Mind: Why psychiatric treatments fail.* London/New York: Allen Lane.

14. Boyle, M (2002) *Schizophrenia: A scientific delusion?* (2nd ed). London: Routledge.

Chapter 2

1. Greenberg, G (2012) Not diseases but categories of suffering. *New York Times*, 29th January http://www.nytimes.com/2012/01/30/opinion/the-dsms-troubled-revision.html?_r=0

2. Cosgrove, L & Drimsky, L (2012) A comparison of *DSM-IV* and *DSM-5* panel members' financial associations with industry: A pernicious problem persists. *PLoS Medicine, 9*(3), 1–5.

3. Frances, A (2013) Saving normal: An insider's revolt against out-of-control psychiatric diagnosis, *DSM-5*, big pharma and the medicalization of ordinary life. *Psychotherapy in Australia, 19*(3), 14–18. Available online for a very modest fee at http://bit.ly/Yz9TZ2

4. Allen Frances quoted at http://reut.rs/1qpJALu

5. http://www.bps.org.uk/news/society-statement-dsm-5

6. Insel, T (2013) *Director's Blog: Transforming diagnosis*. http://www.nimh.nih.gov/about/director/2013/transforming-diagnosis.shtml

7. Hyman, S (6 May 2013) http://www.nytimes.com/2013/05/07/health/psychiatrys-new-guide-falls-short-experts-say.html?pagewanted=all&_r=0

8. Frances, A (2014) *One Manual Shouldn't Dictate Mental Health Research*. http://www.newscientist.com/article/dn23490-one-manual-shouldnt-dictate-us-mental-health-research.html#.U0_jR3JeF1s

9. Kupfer, D (2013) *Chair of DSM-5 Task Force discusses future of mental health research*. News release, American Psychiatric Association, May 3rd.

10. Page 1 in Division of Clinical Psychology (2013) *Classification of Behaviour and Experience in Relation to Functional Psychiatric Diagnoses: Time for a paradigm shift*. Leicester: British Psychological Society. Available from http://shop.bps.org.uk/classification-of-behaviour-and-experience-in-relation-to-functional-psychiatric-diagnoses-time-for-a-paradigm-shift.html

11. Greenberg, G (2010) *Inside the Battle to Define Mental Illness*. http://www.wired.com/2010/12/ff_dsmv

12. Page 439 in Oyebode, F & Humphries, M (2011) The future of psychiatry. *British Journal of Psychiatry, 199,* 439–40.

Chapter 3

1. https://www.youtube.com/watch?v=GUMY5NUhVTU

2. Read, J & Sanders, P (2010) *A Straight Talking Introduction to the Causes of Mental Health Problems.* Ross-on-Wye: PCCS Books.

Endnotes pp. 10–19

3. Gerhardt, S (2004) *Why Love Matters: How affection shapes a baby's brain.* Hove: Brunner-Routledge.

4. See n. 2.

5. Page 3 in Sharfstein, S (2005) Big Pharma and American psychiatry: The good, the bad and the ugly. *Psychiatric News, 40*(16), 3. Available at http://psychnews.psychiatryonline.org/newsArticle.aspx?articleid=109213

6. Page 505 in Breggin, P (1993) *Toxic Psychiatry.* London: Fontana.

7. Kovel, J (1980) The American mental health industry. In D Ingleby (ed) *Critical Psychiatry: The politics of mental health* (pp 72–101). Harmondsworth: Penguin.

8. Boyle, M (1999) Diagnosis. In C Newnes, G Holmes & C Dunn (eds) *This Is Madness: A critical look at psychiatry and the future of mental health services* (pp 75–90). Ross-on-Wye: PCCS Books.

9. Goodwin, GM & Geddes, JR (2007) What is the heartland of psychiatry? *British Journal of Psychiatry, 191,* 189–91.

10. American Psychiatric Association (1987) *Diagnostic and Statistical Manual of Mental Disorders* (3rd ed, rev) (*DSM-III-R*). Washington DC: American Psychiatric Association.

11. Kirk, SA & Kutchins, H (1997) *Making Us Crazy: DSM – The psychiatric bible and the creation of mental disorder*. New York/London: The Free Press.

12. Page 44 in Lewis, G & Appleby, L (1988) The patients psychiatrists dislike. *British Journal of Psychiatry, 153,* 44–9.

13. See n. 11.

14. Timimi, S (2011, 21 May) *No More Psychiatric Labels*. Available at http://www.criticalpsychiatry.net/?p=527

15. Mirowsky, J (1990) Subjective boundaries and combinations in psychiatric diagnosis. *Journal of Mind and Behavior, 11,* 161–78.

16. Laing, RD & Esterson, A (1964) *Sanity, Madness and the Family*. London: Tavistock Press.

Szasz, T (1961) *The Myth of Mental Illness.* New York: Harper and Row.

Szasz, T (1976) Schizophrenia: The sacred symbol of psychiatry. *British Journal of Psychiatry, 129,* 308–16.

17. Read, J, Johnstone, L & Taitimu, M (2013) Psychosis, poverty and ethnicity. In J Read & J Dillon (eds) *Models of Madness: Psychological, social and biological approaches to psychosis* (2nd ed) (pp 191–209). London/New York: Routledge.

18. Fernando, S (2002) *Mental Health, Race and Culture* (2nd ed). Basingstoke/New York: Palgrave.

19. See n. 14.

20. Watters, E (2011) *Crazy Like Us: The globalization of the Western mind.* London: Constable & Robinson.

21. Page 56 in Kirk & Kutchins, 1997. See n. 11.

22. Proctor, G (2007) Disordered boundaries? A critique of 'borderline personality disorder'. In H Spandler & S Warner (eds) *Beyond Fear and Control: Working with young people who self-harm* (*A 42nd Street reader*) (pp 105–19). Ross-on-Wye: PCCS Books.

23. Page 112 in Proctor, 2007. See n. 22.

Chapter 4

1. Moncrieff, J (2009) *A Straight Talking Introduction to Psychiatric Drugs.* Ross-on-Wye: PCCS Books.

2. Page 13 in Moncrieff, 2009. See n. 1.

3. Timimi, S (2011, 21 May) *No More Psychiatric Labels*. Available at http://www.criticalpsychiatry.net/?p=527

4. Romme, M & Escher, S (2000) *Making Sense of Voices: A guide for mental health professionals.* London: Mind Publications.

5. Whitaker, R (2010) *Anatomy of an Epidemic: Magic bullets, psychiatric drugs, and the astonishing rise of mental illness in America.* New York: Crown Publishing Group.

6. Page 7 in Craddock, N et al (2008) Wake-up call for British psychiatry. *British Journal of Psychiatry, 193,* 6–9.

7. Page 11 in Wessely, S (2013) The idea that there is a conspiracy is frankly laughable. *The Observer* 12th May. Available at http://www.theguardian.com/science/2013/may/12/dsm-5-conspiracy-laughable

8. Interview with Professor Nick Craddock. http://www.bbc.co.uk/programmes/p0195g8k

9. Read, J & Sanders, P (2010) *A Straight Talking Introduction to the Causes of Mental Health Problems.* Ross-on-Wye: PCCS Books.

10. Read, J & Bentall, RP (2012) Negative childhood experiences and mental health: Theoretical, clinical and primary prevention implications. *British Journal of Psychiatry, 200,* 89–91.

Chapter 5

1. Parsons, T (1951) Illness and the role of the physician: A sociological perspective. *American Journal of Orthopsychiatry, 21,* 452–60.

2. Scott, RD (1973a) The treatment barrier: Part 1. *British Journal of Medical Psychology, 46,* 45–55.

Scott, RD (1973b) The treatment barrier: Part 2. *British Journal of Medical Psychology, 46,* 57–67.

3. Honos-Webb, L & Leitner, LM (2001) How using the *DSM* causes damage: A client's report. *Journal of Humanistic Psychology, 41*(4), 36–56.

4. Kemp, J, Lickel, J & Deacon, B (2014) Effects of a chemical imbalance causal explanation on individuals' perceptions of their depressive symptoms. *Behaviour Research and Therapy.* Online March 6, 2014. http://dx.doi.org/10.1016/j.brat.2014.02.009

5. Page 17 in Beresford, P (2010) *A Straight Talking Introduction to Being a Mental Health Service User.* Ross-on-Wye: PCCS Books.

6. McCabe, R, Heath, C, Burns, T & Priebe, S (2002) Engagement of patients with psychosis in the consultation. *British Medical Journal, 325,* 1148–51.

7. Page 57 in Georgaca, E (2013) Social constructionist contributions to critiques of psychiatric diagnosis and classification. *Feminism and Psychology, 23*(1), 56–62.

8. Terkelson, TB (2009) Transforming the subjectivities of psychiatric care. *Subjectivity, 27,* 195–216.

9. Colombo, A, Bendelow, G, Fulford, B & Williams, S (2003) Evaluating the influence of implicit models of mental disorder on processes of shared decision-making within community-based mental health teams. *Social Science and Medicine, 56,* 1557–70.

10. Page 112 in Hood, N, Johnstone, L & Christofides, S (2013) The hidden solution? Staff experiences, views and understanding of the use of psychological formulation in multi-disciplinary teams. *Journal of Critical Psychology, Counselling and Psychotherapy, 13*(2), 107–16.

11. Johnstone, L (1993) Psychiatry: Are we allowed to disagree? *Clinical Psychology Forum, 56,* 19–22 (reprinted in *Clinical Psychology Forum, 100,* 1997).

12. Jacqui Dillon (20th May 2013) at http://www.madinamerica.com/2013/05/hearing-voices-network-launches-debate-on-dsm-5-and-psychiatric-diagnoses

13. Time to Change (2008) *Stigma Shout: Service user and carer experiences of stigma and discrimination.* http://www.time-to-change.org.uk/sites/default/files/Stigma%20Shout.pdf

14. Cowan, L & Hart, D (1998) Changing minds. Every family in the land: A new challenge for the future (editorial). *Psychiatric Bulletin, 22,* 593–4. Kvaale EP, et al.

15. Read, J, Haslam, N & Magliano, L (2013) Prejudice, stigma and 'schizophrenia': The role of bio-genetic ideology. In J Read and J Dillon (eds) *Models of Madness: Psychological, social and biological approaches to psychosis* (2nd ed) (pp 157–77). London/New York: Routledge.

16. Angermeyer, MC, Holzinger, A, Carta, MG & Schomerus, G (2011) Biogenetic explanations and public acceptance of mental illness: Systematic review of population studies. *British Journal of Psychiatry, 199,* 367–72.

17. Kvaale, EP, Gottdiener, WH & Haslam, N (2013) Biogenetic explanations and stigma: A meta-analytic review of associations among laypeople. *Social Science and Medicine, 96,* 95–103.

18. See n. 15.

Chapter 6

1. Page 260 in Horn, N, Johnstone, L & Brooke, S (2007) Some service user perspectives on the diagnosis of borderline personality disorder. *Journal of Mental Health, 16*(2), 255–69.

2. Page 366 in Shooter, M (2010) What my diagnosis means to me. *Journal of Mental Health, 19*(4), 366–8.

3. Page 366 in Shooter, 2010. See n. 2.

4. Page 10, quote from Terry, in Rethink (2010) *Recovery Insights: Learning from lived experience.* London: Rethink. http://www.rethink.org/resources/r/recovery-insights_

5. Fay Thomas at http://discursiveoftunbridgewells.blogspot.co.uk/2013/09/the-lament-of-black-swan-i-dont-need-my.html#more

6. Page 161 in Maree, L, Inder, ML, Crowe, MT, Joyce, PR, Moor, S, Carter, JD & Luty, SE (2010) 'I really don't know whether it is still there': Ambivalent acceptance of a diagnosis of bipolar disorder. *Psychiatric Quarterly, 81,* 157–65.

7. Page 366 in Shooter, 2010. See n. 2.

8. Page 236 in Bilderbeck, AC, Saunders, KEA, Price, J & Goodwin, GM (2014) Psychiatric assessment of mood instability: Qualitative study of patient experience. *British Journal of Psychiatry, 204,* 234–9.

9. Page 421 in Pitt, L, Kilbride, M, Welford, M, Nothard, S & Morrison, AP (2009) Impact of a dx of psychosis: User-led qualitative study. *Psychiatric Bulletin, 33,* 419–23.

10. Page 32 in Division of Clinical Psychology (2010) *Understanding Bipolar Disorder: Why some people experience extreme mood states and what can help.* Leicester: British Psychological Society.

11. Page 32 in Hornstein, GA (2013) Whose account matters? *Feminism and Psychology, 23*(1), 29–40.

12. Sally Edwards, quoted in Division of Clinical Psychology, *Understanding 'Psychosis'.* Leicester: British Psychological Society (due in late 2014). Will be available at http://shop.bps.org.uk

13. Page 119 in Romme, M, Escher, S, Dillon, D, Corstens, D & Morris, M (eds) (2009) *Living with Voices: 50 stories of recovery.* Ross-on-Wye: PCCS Books.

14. Page 261 in Horn et al, 2007. See n. 1.

15. Page 529 in Callard, F (2014) Psychiatric diagnosis: The indispensability of ambivalence. *Journal of Medical Ethics, 40*(8), 526–30.

16. Page 529 in Callard, 2014. See n. 15.

17. Page 22 in Campbell, P (2010) Surviving the system. In T Basset & S Stickley (eds) *Voices of Experience: Narratives of mental health survivors.* Chichester: Wiley-Blackwell.

18. See n. 9.

19. Page 723 in Hayne, YM (2003) Experiencing psychiatric diagnosis: Client perspectives on being named mentally ill. *Journal of Psychiatric and Mental Health Nursing, 10,* 722–9.

20. Page 75 in Barham P & Hayward R (1995) *Relocating Madness: From the mental patient to the person.* London: Free Association Press.

21. Laura Delano at http://www.madinamerica.com/2010/10/chapter-two-opening-pandoras-box/

22. Page 723 in Hayne, 2003. See n. 19.

23. Page 723 in Hayne, 2003. See n. 19.

24. Page 40 in Honos-Webb, L & Leitner, LM (2001) How using the DSM causes damage: A client's report. *Journal of Humanistic Psychology, 41*(4), 36–56.

25. Lindow, V (1992) A service user's perspective. In H Wright & M Goddey (eds) *Mental Health Nursing: From first principles to professional practice.* London: Chapman and Hall.

26. Page 217 in Knight, MTD, Wykes, T & Hayward, P (2003) People don't understand: An investigation of schizophrenia using Interpretative Phenomenological Analysis (IPA). *Journal of Mental Health, 12*(3), 209–22.

27. Page 214 in Knight et al, 2003. See n. 26.

28. Page 537 in Corrigan, PW & Miller, FE (2004) Shame, blame and contamination: A review of the impact of mental illness stigma on family members. *Journal of Mental Health, 13*(6), 537–48.

29. Page 540 in Corrigan & Miller, 2004. See n. 28.

30. Fay Thomas at http://discursiveoftunbridgewells.blogspot.co.uk/2013/06/am-i-still-bipolar-emerging-from-shadow.html

31. Wilton Hall at http://psychdiagnosis.weebly.com/stories-of-harm.html

32. Page 216 in Knight et al, 2003. See n. 26.

33. Anonymous 1 at http://psychdiagnosis.weebly.com/stories-of-harm.html

Endnotes pp. 66–72

34. Wilton Hall at http://psychdiagnosis.weebly.com/stories-of-harm.html

35. Janie Lee at http://psychdiagnosis.weebly.com/stories-of-harm.html

36. Janie Lee at http://psychdiagnosis.weebly.com/stories-of-harm.html

37. Page 337 in Parry, P (2014) Biologism in psychiatry: A young man's experience of being diagnosed with 'pediatric bipolar disorder'. *Journal of Clinical Medicine, 3,* 334–47.

38. Page 210 in Knight et al, 2003. See n. 26.

39. Page 421 in Pitt et al, 2009. See n. 9.

40. Page 214 in Knight et al, 2003. See n. 26.

41. Page 76 in Barham & Hayward, 1995. See n. 20.

42. Page 66 in Bradfield, BC (2002) *The Phenomenology of Psychiatric Diagnosis.* Unpublished MA thesis, University of Rhodes, South Africa.

43. Page 262 in Horn et al, 2007. See n. 1.

44. Page 262 in Horn et al, 2007. See n. 1.

45. Page 262 in Horn et al, 2007. See n. 1.

46. Page 57 in Castillo, H (2000) Temperament or trauma? Users' views on the nature and treatment of personality disorder. *Mental Health Care, 4*(21), 53–8.

47. Page 237 in Bilderbeck et al, 2014. See n. 8.

48. Leeming, D, Boyle, M & MacDonald, J (2009) Accounting for psychological problems: How user-friendly are psychosocial formulations? *Clinical Psychology Forum, 200,* 12–17.

49. Laura Delano at http://www.madinamerica.com/2010/11/chapter-three-at-war-with-a-diagnosis/

50. See n. 30.

51. Sally Edwards. See n. 12.

Chapter 7

1. Page 32 in Hornstein, GA (2013) Whose account matters? *Feminism and Psychology, 23*(1), 29–40.

2. Anthony, WA (1993) Recovery from mental illness: The guiding vision of the mental health system in the 1990s. *Innovation and Research, 2,* 17–24.

3. HM Government (2009) *New Horizons: A shared vision for mental health.* London: Department of Health.

4. Andresen, R, Oades, L, & Caputi, P (2003) The experience of recovery from schizophrenia: Towards an empirically validated stage model. *Australian and New Zealand Journal of Psychiatry, 37*(5), 586–93.

5. Leamy, M, Bird, V, Le Boutillier, C, Williams, J & Slade, M (2011) Conceptual framework for personal recovery in mental health: Systematic review and narrative synthesis. *British Journal of Psychiatry, 199,* 445–52.

6. Warner, R (2010) Does the scientific evidence support the recovery model? *The Psychiatrist, 34,* 3–5.

7. Pages 69–70 in Beresford, P (2010) *A Straight Talking Introduction to Being a Mental Health Service User.* Ross-on-Wye: PCCS Books.

8. Page xiv in Bentall, RP (2009) *Doctoring the Mind: Why psychiatric treatments fail.* London/New York: Allen Lane.

9. See n. 7.

10. Dillon, J, Johnstone, L & Longden, E (2012) Trauma, dissociation, attachment and neuroscience: A new paradigm for understanding severe mental distress. *Journal of Critical Psychology, Counselling and Psychotherapy, 12*(3), 145–55.

11. An information leaflet on dissociation can be downloaded from MIND at http://www.mind.org.uk/information-support/types-of-mental-health-problems/dissociative-disorders/?gclid=CMCdvJ7y9r0CFQUFwwodVRcAuA

12. Page 261 in Wilkinson, R & Pickett, K (2009) *The Spirit Level: Why more equal societies almost always do better.* London: Allen Lane.

13. Hesse, E (2008) The adult attachment interview: Protocol, method of analysis and empirical studies. In J Cassidy & PR Shaver (eds) *Handbook of Attachment: Theory, research and clinical implications* (pp 552–98). London/New York: Guilford Press.

14. Neuner, F, Catani, C, Ruf, M, Schauer, E, Schauer, M & Elbert, T (2008) Narrative exposure therapy for the treatment of traumatized children and adolescents (KidNET): From neurocognitive theory to field intervention. *Child and Adolescent Psychiatric Clinics of North America, 17*(3), 641–64.

15. Romme, M & Escher, S (2000) *Making Sense of Voices: A guide for mental health professionals.* London: Mind Publications.

16. Page 123, S Brison quoted in Thomas, P & Longden, E (2013) Madness, childhood adversity and narrative psychiatry: Caring and the moral imagination. *Medical Humanities, 39,* 119–25.

17. Johnstone, L & Dallos, R (2013) *Formulation in Psychology and Psychotherapy: Making sense of people's problems* (2nd ed). London/New York: Routledge.

18. Page 8 in Harper, D & Moss, D (2003) A different chemistry? Re-formulating formulation. *Clinical Psychology, 25,* 6–10.

19. Page 2 in Butler, G (1998) Clinical formulation. In AS Bellack and M Hersen (eds) *Comprehensive Clinical Psychology, Vol 6* (pp 1–24). Oxford: Pergamon.

20. Johnstone, L (2013) Using formulation in teams. In Johnstone & Dallos, 2013. See n. 17.

21. Division of Clinical Psychology (2011) *Good Practice Guidelines on the Use of Psychological Formulation.* Leicester: British Psychological Society. Can be downloaded from http://shop.bps.org.uk/good-practice-guidelines-on-the-use-of-psychological-formulation.html

22. Division of Clinical Psychology (2011). See n. 21.

23. Page 29 in Division of Clinical Psychology (2011). See n. 21.

24. Page 20 in Division of Clinical Psychology (2011). See n. 21.

25. Royal College of Psychiatrists (2010) *A Competency Based Curriculum for Specialist Core Training in Psychiatry.* Retrieved 5th October 2011 from www.rcpsych.ac.uk/training/curriculum2010.aspx

26. Page 29 in Division of Clinical Psychology (2011). See n. 21.

27. Page 17 in Division of Clinical Psychology (2011). See n. 21.

28. Page 16 in Romme & Escher (2000). See n. 15.

29. Page 29 in Romme & Escher (2000). See n. 15.

30. Johnstone, L (2012) Voice hearers are people with problems, not patients with illnesses. In M Romme & S Escher (eds) *Psychosis as a Personal Crisis.* London/New York: Routledge.

31. Knight, T (2013) *Beyond Belief: Alternative ways of working with delusions, obsessions and unusual experiences.* Peter Lehmann Publishing. Downloadable free from http://www.peter-lehmann-publishing.com/beyond-belief.htm

32. Rachel Waddingham (2013) *Symptom or Experience: Does language matter?* http://www.madinamerica.com/2013/08/does-language-matter

33. Fay Thomas at http://discursiveoftunbridgewells.blogspot.co.uk/2013/06/am-i-still-bipolar-emerging-from-shadow.html

34. Page 16 in Dillon, J & May, R (2003) Reclaiming experience. *Openmind, 120,* 16–17.

35. Rowe, D (1990) Introduction. In J Masson *Against Therapy.* London: Fontana.

Chapter 8

1. Page 311 in Romme M, Escher S, Dillon D, Corstens D & Morris, M (eds) (2009) *Living with Voices: 50 stories of recovery.* Ross-on-Wye: PCCS Books.

2. Page 95 in James, A (2001) *Raising our Voices: An account of the Hearing Voices Movement.* Gloucester: Handsell Publishing.

3. Longden, E (2010): Making sense of voices: A personal story of recovery. *Psychosis: Psychological, Social and Integrative Approaches, 2*(3), 255–9.

4. Rufus May, pages 292–4 in Romme et al (2009). See n. 1.

5. These extracts from Laura Delano's story are from two sources:
http://www.madinamerica.com/2013/02/reflections-on-a-psychiatric-indoctrination-or-how-i-began-to-free-myself-from-the-cult-of-psychiatry

https://m.facebook.com/lfdelano/posts/10101255431631741

6. Page 181 in Herman, JL (1997) *Trauma and Recovery: From domestic abuse to political terror.* New York: Basic Books.

7. Page 122 in Thomas, P & Longden, E (2013) Madness, childhood adversity and narrative psychiatry: Caring and the moral imagination. *Medical Humanities, 39,* 119–25.

8. Beresford, P (2010) *A Straight Talking Introduction to Being a Mental Health Service User.* Ross-on-Wye: PCCS Books.

9. Page 16 in Dillon, J & May, R (2003) Reclaiming experience. *Openmind, 120,* 16–17.

10. Page 17 in Dillon & May (2003). See n. 9.

Chapter 9

1. Pages 160–1 in Coleman, R (1999) Hearing voices and the politics of oppression. In C Newnes, G Holmes & C Dunn (eds) *This is Madness* (pp 149–63). Ross-on-Wye: PCCS Books.

2. Laura Delano at http://femhc.blogspot.co.uk

3. Louise Gullet at http://www.schizophreniacommission.org.uk/commissioner-blogs/personal-perspectives

4. Page 294 in Romme, M, Escher, S, Dillon, D, Corstens, D & Morris, M (eds) (2009) *Living with Voices: 50 stories of recovery.* Ross-on-Wye: PCCS Books.

5. Phil Thomas at http://www.madinamerica.com/2012/09/narrative-psychiatry-a-review

6. Moncrieff, J (2009) *A Straight Talking Introduction to Psychiatric Drugs.* Ross-on-Wye: PCCS Books.

7. Statistics from http://www.fph.org.uk/the_cost_of_poor_mental_health

8. Whitaker, R (2010) *Anatomy of an Epidemic: Magic bullets, psychiatric drugs, and the astonishing rise of mental illness in America.* New York: Crown Publishing Group.

9. Chapter 10 in Johnstone, L (2000) *Users and Abusers of Psychiatry: A critical look at psychiatric practice* (2nd ed). Hove, New York: Routledge. An accessible overview of the limitations of current practice, illustrated by real-life examples.

10. Chapter 7 in Johnstone (2000). See n. 9.

11. http://opendialogueapproach.co.uk

12. http://www.hearing-voices.org/about-us/position-statement-on-dsm-5/

13. http://www.behindthelabel.co.uk/schizophrenia-commission

Subject Index

Name Index

CPSIA information can be obtained at www.ICGtesting.com
Printed in the USA
LVOW05s1036190115

423422LV00004B/10/P